The Global Future

– Make Your Voice Heard through SDGs –

Junko Kobayashi

English language revisions
Brian Bond

Asahi Press

音声再生アプリ「リスニング・トレーナー」を使った 音声ダウンロード

朝日出版社開発のアプリ、「リスニング・トレーナー（リストレ）」を使えば、教科書の音声を スマホ、タブレットに簡単にダウンロードできます。どうぞご活用ください。

◉ アプリ【リスニング・トレーナー】の使い方

《アプリのダウンロード》

App Store または Google Play から 「リスニング・トレーナー」のアプリ （無料）をダウンロード

App Storeは こちら▶

Google Playは こちら▶

《アプリの使い方》

①アプリを開き「コンテンツを追加」をタップ
②画面上部に【 15717 】を入力しDoneをタップ

音声ストリーミング配信 》》》

この教科書の音声は、 右記ウェブサイトにて 無料で配信しています。

https://text.asahipress.com/free/english/

The Global Future – Make Your Voice Heard through SDGs –

Cover design: Masaaki Kobayashi (ease)
Photograph: Shutterstock, Wikimedia Commons

はしがき

　SDGs は Sustainable Development Goals の略で、「持続可能な開発目標」という説明が不要なくらい、今やこの言葉は広く浸透しています。2015 年に国連サミットで採択され、国連加盟国全てが 2016 年から 2030 年の 15 年間で達成するための目標に掲げていますが、他国ではどのように推進されているのでしょうか。本テキストのリーディングではまず国連での具体的な取り組みに始まり、地方の博物館、個々人の積極的な関与まで、様々な例を採り上げています。その中に、日本人の価値観からプラスの影響を受けたというアメリカ人の発言もあり、日本人が当然視して見過ごしがちな日本的価値観を再発見することにも繋がります。

　グローバル社会で対話力が必要だと指摘されてから久しいのですが、対話力は会話力とは異なり、相手が異なる価値観をもっているというのが前提になります。人間は経験していないことを認識できないので、まず自己と全く異なる経験をし、異なる価値観を持つ人が存在することを知ることから始めましょう。彼らの歴史的背景や置かれている状況を理解すれば、徐々に異なる意見を理解できるようになるでしょう。日頃から異なる価値観を持つ人々の意見に耳を傾け、物事を多角的に捉える能力の養成を目指しましょう。そうすれば、自己と相手との相違点を理解した後、自己の視点を丁寧に説明したり、相手の見解で見倣うべき点を採り入れたりすることによって、グローバル社会で通用する人材になれるのです。

　他国での先進的な取り組みに啓発されて、あなたも SDGs を達成するための活動に積極的に参加することが期待されています。

　この企画に温かいご支援を頂いた朝日出版社社長の小川洋一郎様、編集上の種々のご助言を頂いた編集長の朝日英一郎様と小林啓也様に感謝の意を表します。

著者

Readings

SDGs をテーマにしたエッセイを平易な英文で記してあります。後に続く Notes を参考に読んでみましょう。

Exercises

本文の内容把握の問題、本文と関連した単語や表現の問題、自分の意見をまとめる練習、少人数で意見を交換する訓練、など様々な練習問題が用意されています。

I. Reading Comprehension

本文の大意が正確に把握できているかを確認します。

II. Sentence Completion

本文と関連した単語や表現を採り上げている練習問題を通して、語彙の増強を目指します。

III. Composition

最初に、日本人学生が英語で意見を述べる際によく起こる問題を採り上げ、どのように改良すればよいのか、具体例をあげて説明しています。その例を確認した後、留意すべき点を念頭に置いて、自分自身の意見を述べましょう。

IV. Discussion

最初に議論の例と注意すべき点を採り上げているので、それを参考にしながら、少人数グループに分かれて意見を交換しましょう。そして、個々人の意見は異なるので、自分の意見を他者に分かってもらうためには論理的に説明する必要があることを学びましょう。

Contents

THE 17 GOALS FOR SDGs

SDGs の 17 の目標

GOAL1:　NO POVERTY　貧困をなくそう

GOAL2:　ZERO HUNGER　飢餓をゼロに

GOAL3:　GOOD HEALTH AND WELL-BEING　すべての人に健康と福祉を

GOAL4:　QUALITY EDUCATION　質の高い教育をみんなに

GOAL5:　GENDER EQUALITY　ジェンダー平等を実現しよう

GOAL6:　CLEAN WATER AND SANITATION　安全な水とトイレを世界中に

GOAL7:　AFFORDABLE AND CLEAN ENERGY　エネルギーをみんなに、そしてクリーンに

GOAL8:　DECENT WORK AND ECONOMIC GROWTH　働きがいも経済成長も

GOAL9:　INDUSTORY, INNOVATION AND INFRASTRUCTURE　産業と技術革新の基盤をつくろう

GOAL10: REDUCED INEQUALITIES　人や国の不平等をなくそう

GOAL11: SUSTAINABLE CITIES AND COMMUNITIES　住み続けられるまちづくりを

GOAL12: RESPONSIBLE CONSUMPTION AND PRODUCTION　つくる責任、つかう責任

GOAL13: CLIMATE ACTION　気候変動に具体的な対策を

GOAL14: LIFE BELOW WATER　海の豊かさを守ろう

GOAL15: LIFE ON LAND　陸の豊かさも守ろう

GOAL16: PEACE, JUSTICE AND STRONG INSTITUTIONS　平和と公正をすべての人に

GOAL17: PARTNERSHIPS FOR THE GOALS　パートナーシップで目標を達成しよう

以下のホームページに、各ゴールの詳細がまとめられています。
予習や復習の際に確認して、理解を深めましょう。

国連のホームページ（英語）　　日本ユニセフ協会のホームページ（日本語）

https://sdgs.un.org/goals　　https://www.unicef.or.jp/kodomo/sdgs/

The Global Future

– Make Your Voice Heard through SDGs –

Chapter 1

United Nations' Activities Saving Humanity from Hell

SDGs の目標の内、国連が率先して実践をすることで目まぐるしい成果を上げているのは、貧困地区の子供たちの健康・栄養状態の向上、教育の場の提供です。具体的にどのような活動を行っているのでしょうか。

Readings

It is well known that the term SDGs, standing for sustainable development goals, was adopted at the United Nations' summit, but few people are familiar with the United Nations' specific activities.

Participants in the United Nations' tour were told about the former United Nations Secretary General's statement: "The United Nations was not created 5 to take mankind to heaven, but to save humanity from hell." Then, what specifically has the United Nations done in order to save humanity from hell? While it is hard to imagine the reality for Japanese people who are blessed with a peaceful environment, tens of millions of people have no nationality because of civil wars and ethnic conflicts in the world. They can't go abroad because 10 they don't have their passport. Although the United Nations urges neighboring countries to accept those people, few nations can afford to accept them. It is UNICEF standing for the United Nations International Children's Emergency Fund that has achieved remarkable results regarding assistance to these people. UNICEF has created an educational environment and has donated 15 boxes of stationery for refugee children so that they can receive education. Also, UNICEF has collected donations for people in developing countries, has improved the nutritional status of children and has provided vaccinations against diseases. UNICEF has certainly saved those children who are in hell.

People's opinions are divided on whether the United Nations plays an 20 important role in international relations. A tour guide of the United Nations explained that at first economic sanctions are imposed on nations that violate international agreements, but when the sanctions have no effect, military operations are approved. However, resolutions by the United Nations have no binding power. There is some doubt left about effective solutions toward 25 violations such as frequent missile launches by North Korea. Many participants in the tour said, "The United Nations has done a wonderful job of saving underprivileged people, to be sure, but the United Nations is powerless concerning conflict resolution."

As the above example indicates, we need to examine activities of one 30 organization from various angles. It is dangerous to judge the activities simply as good or evil. It is important to judge activities after analyzing them from various viewpoints; for instance, the activities have achieved good results in such and such fields, but there is some room for improvement in such and such points. 35

Notes

l.1 **SDGs:** 持続可能な開発目標 / l.3 **specific activities:** 具体的な活動 / l.5 **Secretary General:** 事務総長 / l.8 **reality:** 現実 / l.9 **nationality:** 国籍 / l.10 **civil wars:** 内戦 / l.10 **ethnic conflicts:** 民族対立 / l.13 **UNICEF:** ユニセフ / l.16 **stationery:** 文房具 / l.16 **refugee children:** 難民の子供たち / l.17 **donations:** 寄付金 / l.18 **nutritional status:** 栄養状態 / l.18 **vaccinations:** 予防注射 / l.22 **economic sanctions:** 経済制裁 / l.22 **violate:** 〜に違反する / l.23 **military operations:** 軍事行動 / l.24 **be approved:** 承認される / l.24 **resolutions:** 決議 / l.25 **binding power:** 拘束力 / l.26 **launches:** 発射 / l.28 **underprivileged people:** 恵まれない人々 / l.28 **powerless:** 無力な / l.29 **conflict resolution:** 紛争解決 / l.32 **good:** 善 / l.32 **evil:** 悪

Exercises 1

I. Reading Comprehension

Questions are based on the content of the text. Choose the best answer.

1. Are people familiar with the United Nations' activities?

    (A) Most people are not familiar with the specific activities.

    (B) Many people are familiar only with the political activities.

    (C) Only people in developed nations are familiar with the activities.

    (D) The majority of people have a clear understanding of the activities.

2. What is the point of the former United Nations Secretary's statement?

    (A) The United Nations should aim at making people happy.

    (B) The United Nations should educate people so that they can go to heaven.

    (C) The United Nations should focus on people suffering from poverty.

    (D) The United Nations should treat people equally all the time.

3. Why don't a large number of people have passports?

    (A) They frequently move from one place to another.

    (B) After living abroad for a long time, they have lost it.

    (C) Dictatorships have deprived some people of their passports.

    (D) Conflicts and wars are caused in their country.

4. What did many tour participants agree on?

    (A) Economic sanctions by the United Nations are effective.

    (B) The United Nations has effective measures to tackle poverty.

    (C) Resolutions by the United Nations are effective.

    (D) The United Nations has outstanding political power.

5. What should we pay attention to when judging one organization's activities?

    (A) We should pass judgment on good or evil with clear reasons.

    (B) We should pass judgment considering political power.

    (C) We should form judgment without being affected by others.

    (D) We should form judgment considering diverse points.

II. Sentence Completion

Adverbs, adverbial phrases and clauses（副詞、副詞句、副詞節）

Choose the best answer as a synonym of the word(s) given in the bracket.

1. UNICEF has created an educational environment for refugee children
   _____ they can receive education. (with a purpose)

   (A) so much   (B) so long

   (C) so as to   (D) so that

2. UNICEF has _____ saved refugee children who are in hell. (surely)

   (A) certainly   (B) partially

   (C) only   (D) merely

3. _____ economic sanctions are imposed on countries that violate international
   agreements. (Initially)

   (A) First of all   (B) At first

   (C) For the first time   (D) First thing

4. The United Nations plays a leading role in helping poor people, _____, but it
   is not politically powerful. (certainly)

   (A) maybe   (B) probably

   (C) to be sure   (D) absolutely

5. It is not a wise policy to judge one organization's activities _____ by good or
   evil. (just)

   (A) similarly   (B) simply

   (C) simultaneously   (D) silently

反対意見を述べる際には、まず相手の意見に理解を示しましょう！

意見が対立した場合、まず相手の言い分に耳を傾けていることを示しましょう！その時に
使えるのが構文 "... to be sure, but..."（なるほど ... ですが ...）です。例えば、以下のよう
に用います。
"It's an interesting project, to be sure, but we have to cut down on the expenses. Is it
possible to reduce the expenses in the project? "
（なるほど面白い企画ですが、経費を削減しなければなりません。その企画で経費を削減
することは可能ですか）
このように用いることで、たとえ反対意見であっても、相手に聞いてもらい易くなります。

III. Composition

Practice organizing your ideas based on what you have learned through reading. Remember that each person has different opinions and you have to give a detailed explanation.

1. What have you learned through reading about education?

   ex. I have learned that many children can't receive education.

   [Points for improvement]
   Mention how you have changed your view about education.

   [The revised answer]
   I have learned that many children can't receive education. Although I took education for granted, I have realized that I'm blessed with the present educational environment.

   ....

   ....

   ....

   ....

   ....

   ....

   ....

   ....

   ....

   ....

2. What have you learned through reading about nutrition or vaccinations?

   ....

   ....

   ....

   ....

   ....

   ....

   ....

   ....

   ....

   ....

IV. Discussion

Practice expressing your opinions clearly. Have your own discussion using the sample below as a reference.

1. **What do you think about the present government's policies?**

Sample discussion

A: What do you think about the present government's policies?

B: I think it is appropriate to increase defense costs in terms of the present world situation, but other policies need reconsidering.

A: Can you give me a specific example for the latter statement?

B: For example, I think the government should spend more money on doctors and nurses because they have taken on more responsibility since the spread of coronavirus.

A: So do I. I think the government should spend more money on caregivers as well.

[Notes] **defense costs:** 防衛費　**caregivers:** 介護士

2. **What do you think about policies in your hometown?**

相手によって表現を使い分け、積極的に発言をしましょう！

英語による議論では、黙って傾聴することは評価されません。相手の発言に対して積極的に質問し、興味を示すことが求められます。その際、尋ねる相手によって表現を変えましょう。

友達など親しい人の場合
"Can you give me a specific example?"
（具体例をあげてもらえますか）

目上の人の場合
"Would you give me a specific example?"
（具体例をあげて頂けますか）

相手の意見に賛成する場合も、**"So do I."**（私もそうです）で終わらせるだけではなく、相手の意見を補足するなどして、話題を発展させるように工夫をしましょう。

Chapter 2 Slavery as Big Business

奴隷制度は過去のものと思っている人が多いようですが、現在でも形を変えて存在しており、奴隷状態での労働を強いられている子供たちの数は少なくありません。彼らの存在を知って、巷で見かける製品が正当な労働契約の下で作られたものかどうか、考えてみましょう。

Readings

When buying products, many people value the price of products. Consequently, large-scale stores whose selling points are low prices have picked up momentum. However, if consumers take into account the background in which items are produced, they may change their attitude toward choosing items. 5

The National Center for Civil and Human Rights which opened in Atlanta, the southern part of the United States in 2014 provides visitors with an opportunity to consider human rights from various angles. What impressed me strongly is a video on children who suffered under slavery. With a sensational message: "Slavery is big business," the video broadcasts harsh 10 working conditions of many children in developing countries. Although they are forced to work long hours in a terrible working environment, their wages are extremely low. A social worker visiting the museum mentioned the present conditions. "I have realized through my longtime experiences that people need jobs, not social welfare. I have negotiated with governmental officers over financial aid to secure employment. Before the implementation of the plan, many companies transferred their factories to developing countries in order to cut down on production expenses. Some companies tried to take on children in order to reduce personnel expenses further."

Companies have transferred factories to developing countries in order to live up to the needs of consumers who prefer purchasing products at as low prices as possible. Consequently, it has caused a vicious circle: Children in developing countries have suffered under slavery and the number of unemployed people in developed nations has been remarkably increasing. This vicious circle applies to groceries in particular. Organically grown vegetables and grass-fed livestock are relatively high in price. Because of the low price, many consumers purchase foreign vegetables grown with agricultural chemicals and foreign meat preserved in formalin.

One exhibit at the above museum implied a solution: "We need to make sure companies don't use slave labor that carries their brands." In order to break through this vicious circle, consumers have to become aware of the background in which items are produced and recognize that they should pay a price appropriate for employee labor. Each consumer's choice can be a catalyst for social change.

Notes

l.3 **momentum:** 勢い / l.6 **The National Center for Civil and Human Rights:** 国立公民権・人権博物館 / l.9 **slavery:** 奴隷状態（制度）/ l.10 **harsh:** 過酷な / l.12 **terrible:** 劣悪な / l.15 **social welfare:** 社会福祉 / l.16 **financial aid:** 財政援助 / l.16 **employment:** 雇用 / l.16 **implementation:** 実行 / l.17 **transfer:** 〜を移転する / l.18 **production expenses:** 生産費 / l.19 **personnel expenses:** 人件費 / l.21 **consumers:** 消費者 / l.22 **vicious circle:** 悪循環 / l.25 **groceries:** 食料品 / l.26 **livestock:** 家畜 / l.27 **agricultural chemicals:** 農薬 / l.33 **catalyst:** 起爆剤

Exercises 2

I. Reading Comprehension

Questions are based on the content of the text. Choose the best answer.

1. **What is common consumer behavior?**
    (A) Only people in developed countries look for famous brands.
    (B) Only young people try to look for fashionable items.
    (C) The quality of products is more important than the price.
    (D) The price of products is more important than the quality.

2. **What can visitors to the museum recognize?**
    (A) Slavery existed in the past.
    (B) Slavery still exists in different forms today.
    (C) Slavery is not related to business.
    (D) Slavery is not profit-driven.

3. **What did the social worker believe?**
    (A) Social welfare should be developed for everyone.
    (B) Financial aid should be offered to unemployed people.
    (C) Creating employment is very important.
    (D) Hiring more children is necessary.

4. **What is the tendency of many consumers?**
    (A) They are interested in organic food and healthy livestock.
    (B) They worry about the influence of formalin on their health.
    (C) They are concerned about the effect of agricultural chemicals.
    (D) They pay attention to the price of vegetables and meat.

5. **What is expected of each consumer to change society for the better?**
    (A) To buy products at a reasonable price.
    (B) To hold political demonstrations against slave labor.
    (C) To ask company managers to transfer their factories back to their home country.
    (D) To urge factory supervisors to have children work in better conditions.

II. Sentence Completion

Idioms（慣用句）

Choose the best answer as a synonym of the word(s) given in the bracket.

1. Large-scale stores have _____ momentum. (gained)

    (A) picked up   (B) picked out
    (C) picked on   (D) picked off

2. Companies have to _____ the needs of consumers. (meet)

    (A) look up to   (B) live up to
    (C) live on   (D) look over

3. Many companies tried to _____ production expenses. (reduce)

    (A) cut out   (B) cut off
    (C) cut through   (D) cut down on

4. Some companies tried to _____ children. (employ)

    (A) take over   (B) take on
    (C) take off   (D) take up

5. We have to _____ this vicious circle. (overcome)

    (A) break through   (B) break up
    (C) break out   (D) break off

---

pick up のいろいろな用法

普段の会話で、「大事な点をピックアップしてまとめました」と言うことがあると思いますが、この「ピックアップ」は和製英語であり、英語では "pick up" ではなく、"pick out" を用います。例えば、**"I picked out important items and organized them."** とするのが正しい用法です。

"pick up" は他にも、**"pick up momentum"**（勢いづく）や **"I pick up trash on the beach as a volunteer activity."**（ボランティア活動として海岸のゴミを集めています）、**"I picked up some Spanish when traveling abroad."**（海外旅行でスペイン語を聞き覚えました）といった使い方があります。

新しく出会った表現は、和製英語かどうか辞書を引いて用例を確認してみましょう。

III. Composition

Practice organizing your ideas based on what you have learned through reading. Remember that each person has different opinions and you have to give a detailed explanation.

1. **What have you learned through reading about the production process?**

   ex. I have learned that children in developing nations are forced to work in a terrible working environment.

   [Points for improvement]

   Mention how you have changed your view about the selection of products.

   [The revised answer]

   I have learned that many children in developing nations are forced to work in a terrible working environment, so I have decided to buy products from ethically responsible companies.

   [Notes] ethically responsible companies: 倫理的に信頼できる会社

   ....

   ....

   ....

   ....

   ....

   ....

   ....

   ....

2. **What have you learned through reading about groceries?**

   ....

   ....

   ....

   ....

   ....

   ....

   ....

   ....

   ....

   ....

IV. Discussion

Practice expressing your opinions clearly. Have your own discussion using the sample below as a reference.

1. Organize your ideas concerning grocery security based on your direct experiences or indirect experiences such as through books or magazines.

   [Notes] grocery security: 食の安全

Sample discussion

A: Have you ever considered grocery security to be different from what you thought?

B: Yes, I thought that every government test agricultural chemicals to see if they are safe, but the other day I found out through a book that the benchmarks are greatly different from country and country.

A: Do you mean that if we eat foods grown abroad, we can't tell if they are safe?

B: I'm afraid so. More agricultural chemicals may be used on food imported from abroad.

A: Thank you for sharing important information with me. We cannot be too careful when choosing foods.

[Notes] agricultural chemicals: 農薬（**drugs** を使うと麻薬になるので注意が必要）
benchmarks: 基準

2. Organize inconvenient incidents you have personally experienced due to the spread of coronavirus and point out the risk of depending on foreign countries for producing items.

相手の意図を確認する表現

相手と自分の理解が同じかどうか確かめたい場合には、**"Do you mean ...?"**（～を意味しているのですか）を使って確認しましょう。聞かれた側は、応答が相手にとって好ましくない場合、事務的な応答の **"Yes, I do."** は避けて、**"I'm afraid so."**（残念ながらそうです）と応じ、さらに説明を加えましょう。
尋ねた相手から新しい情報を提供してもらった際には、
"Thank you for sharing important information with me."
（大切な情報を共有してくれて、ありがとうございます）
と続け、感謝の意を表現することが効果的なコミュニケーションの秘訣です。

Chapter 3

Messages Left by Martin Luther King

1960 年代までアメリカ合衆国では人種差別は合法的に行なわれていましたが、キング牧師によって公民権運動が広く展開された結果、1964 年に公民権法が制定され、公正な社会の実現に向けて大きく前進しました。「ブラック・ライブズ・マター」といった運動の存在が示すように人種差別が残る現代、平等な世界を目指す私たちにとっても、キング牧師が残したメッセージは大きな指針となるでしょう。

Readings

Atlanta is the birthplace of a historic figure, Martin Luther King. His name reminds many Americans of his significant contribution to the civil rights movement. Many Americans think that without him, they couldn't have imagined an election of an African-American President.

However, Dr. King didn't carry out the movement only with its focus on 5 African-Americans versus Caucasian-Americans. In order to elicit sympathy from a wide range of people, he had oppressors versus the oppressed in mind. His assertion: "Freedom is never voluntarily given by the oppressor; it must be demanded by the oppressed" clearly indicates his position.

When I interviewed visitors to Dr. King's Center in Atlanta, I found that 10 his assertion won sympathy from a variety of people. An African-American commented on videos and exhibitions. "Our predecessors' voices brought tears to me. I haven't contributed to this movement, but I have benefited a lot from this movement. From now, I will protest against people who have racial prejudice by saying, "What do you get out of that action? I won't use violence. Non-violence will win in the end." Also, a Mexican-American shared his experience. "I was displeased because I was in a disadvantageous position in society. However, now I'm grateful to learn that Dr. King's civil rights movement has secured rights not only for African-Americans but also for other minorities. I have begun to think that I should take the initiative in making requests in the workplace, not just complain about the present situation."

Then, how can people who have no experience with oppression understand the position of the oppressed? I asked a question of a Caucasian man, who was an exception among visitors. "You haven't experienced this type of oppression, have you? What made you become concerned about the civil rights movement?" The man's response was: "I'm a social worker. When I was a child, I lent a hand to elderly people. I always had to consider their needs. I've just transferred the subject from elderly people to minorities. We can foster good relationships only when we understand each other."

It is extremely difficult for human beings to imagine such a situation without any personal experiences. Then, one of the effective solutions is to have men with elite status take part in volunteer activities in areas of poverty and personally experience the situation with the oppressed. Through these experiences, they are expected to direct their attention toward the oppressed.

Notes

l.1 **historic figure:** 歴史上の偉大な人物 / l.2 **significant contribution:** 多大な貢献 / l.2 **civil rights movement:** 公民権運動 / l.4 **African-American President:** アフリカ系アメリカ人大統領 / l.6 **Caucasian-Americans:** 白人のアメリカ人 / l.6 **elicit sympathy:** 共感を引き出す / l.7 **oppressors:** 抑圧者 / l.7 **the oppressed:** 被抑圧者 / l.8 **voluntarily:** 進んで / l.12 **predecessors' voices:** 先人たちの声 / l.13 **benefit:** 恩恵を受ける / l.15 **racial prejudice:** 人種的偏見 / l.16 **non-violence:** 非暴力 / l.20 **minorities:** 少数派の人々 / l.20 **take the initiative:** 率先して〜する / l.28 **subject:** 対象

I. Reading Comprehension

Questions are based on the content of the text. Choose the best answer.

1. **What do many Americans recall when hearing the name of Martin Luther King?**
   (A) They recall his aggressive policies.
   (B) They recall his civil rights movement.
   (C) They think of other historic figures.
   (D) They think of tragedies that happened to historic figures.

2. **What did Dr. King have in mind?**
   (A) He gave priority to the rights of African-Americans.
   (B) He paid special attention to the rights of particular ethnic groups.
   (C) He took the rights of immigrants into account.
   (D) He took the rights of all oppressed people into consideration.

3. **What do the African-American visitor and the Mexican-American visitor have in common?**
   (A) They complain that there is much room for improvement concerning the present situation.
   (B) They are content with their present situation because it is better than it was in the past.
   (C) They think that they should change the present situation on their own initiative.
   (D) They think that they should accept things as they are.

4. **What made the Caucasian-American man become concerned about the civil rights movement?**
   (A) Martin Luther King's speeches did.
   (B) A minority friend of his mother did.
   (C) His experience in his childhood did.
   (D) His association with minorities did.

5. **What do men with elite status need to do?**
   (A) They need to develop their imagination by reading more books.
   (B) They need to watch a variety of movies dealing with social problems.
   (C) They need to collect information on underprivileged districts.
   (D) They need to look at the life of the oppressed with their own eyes.

II. Sentence Completion

Adjectives（形容詞）

Choose the best answer as a synonym of the word(s) given in the bracket.

1. Dr. King paid attention to the _____. (people who are suffering)

   (A) oppressive   (B) oppressor

   (C) oppressed   (D) opposite

2. The Mexican-American was in a / an _____ position. (unfavorable)

   (A) unadvantageous   (B) disadvantageous

   (C) unpleasant   (D) unsatisfactory

3. He is now _____ to learn about the fact. (thankful)

   (A) grateful   (B) grave

   (C) great   (D) gloomy

4. The Caucasian-American man lent a hand to _____ people. (people over 65 years old)

   (A) ancient   (B) elderly

   (C) eager   (D) enthusiastic

5. It is difficult for human beings to imagine a situation without any _____ experiences. (private)

   (A) personal   (B) particular

   (C) specific   (D) vivid

言葉の選択に注意

高齢者と言う時には、"old people（老人）" は好まれません。通常 **"elderly people"** か **"senior citizens"** が用いられます。同じように、アフリカ系アメリカ人は、皮膚の色を表す "black people" ではなく、**"African-Americans"** を使うことを好む人が多いです。

さらに、身障者も "physically handicapped people"（身体に障害のある人）ではなく、**"physically challenged people"**（使える機能を活用して挑戦し続ける人）という表現が用いられるようになっています。

III. Composition

Practice organizing your ideas based on what you have learned through reading. Remember that each person has different opinions and you have to give a detailed explanation.

1. What do you think about the African-American statement: "I haven't contributed to this movement, but I have benefited a lot from this movement"?

   ex. I think it's good.

   [Points for improvement]

   Mention how it is good and how it inspires you.

   [The revised answer]

   It has made me become aware that I haven't contributed to society, either. When an opportunity arises, I would like to help elderly people, for example, to help carry their heavy bags or cross a busy street.

2. What do you think about the Mexican-American remark: "I should take the initiative in making requests in the workplace"?

IV. Discussion

Practice expressing your opinions clearly. Have your own discussion using the sample below as a reference.

1. **It is extremely difficult for human beings to imagine a situation without any personal experiences. Organize what you have discovered through an experience.**

> ### Sample discussion
>
> **A:** Have you experienced that reality is greatly different from what you imagined?
> **B:** Yes, I work as captain of a baseball club. I thought it was easy to unify team members because all of us like baseball. However, I have found it difficult because each member has their own distinct personality.
> **A:** I work as captain of a soccer club, so I know what you mean. When members have made a mistake in a game, some members can get over that quickly while others dwell on that.
> **B:** We have to cheer up the latter type of members by saying, "Never mind."
> **A:** We can also say, "I'm sure that you can bounce back next time!"
>
> **[Notes]** **get over that quickly:** 気持ちをすぐ切り替える　**dwell on that:** 気持ちを引きずる　**Never mind:** 気にしなくていい　**bounce back:** 挽回する

2. **Dr. King is famous for his calm and non-confrontational views. When a person speaks in a condescending tone, no one wants to listen to the statement. Organize your own experience or an experience of someone around you, and mention how you or that person should have conveyed messages more effectively.**

[Notes] non-confrontational: 対立を招かない　in a condescending tone: 上から目線の口調で

> ### 発言への共感と反対意見を述べる時の表現
> 自分自身の同様の経験から相手の発言に共感する場合、次の表現が使えます。
> **"I know what you mean."**（あなたの言うことに同感です）
> 一方、経験からではなく、理論的には理解できる場合は、
> **"I understand what you're saying."**
> （あなたの言わんとしていることは理解できます）
> と言うことができ、この後、下記の例のように反対意見を続けることが多いです。
> **A:** **"There is no use dwelling on the past."**
> （過去のことをくよくよ考えてもしょうがないよ）
> **B:** **"I understand what you're saying, but I still find it difficult to get over that."**
> （言わんとしていることは理解できますが、切り替えるのが難しいのです）

A Remarkable Achievement through Solidarity

社会の不正を是正し、平等な世界を目指すには、人々の協力体制が欠かせません。1950年代のアメリカ合衆国で実際に行われ、公民権運動にもつながったバス・ボイコット運動の成功例から、より公正な社会を目指す上で大切な要因を学びましょう。

Readings

The United States has a lot of museums for African-Americans. The main exhibits are about Martin Luther King and Rose Parks without exception. Her name reminds many Americans of the bus boycott movement by African-Americans. This movement demonstrates that solidarity can achieve noteworthy success even when an individual's power is limited. This has 5 inspired all of the oppressed in the world.

Some museums display bus reproductions with designated seating for Caucasian-Americans only. Rosa Parks questioned this regulation, refused a driver's order to give up her seat to a Caucasian-American and was arrested. People who can imagine the background of the times with African-Americans' 10 blatant segregation can easily understand how courageous her decision was. However, when an elderly African-American curator asked a young African-American visitor, "If you were put in her position, what would you do?" the visitor answered right away, "I would keep sitting in the seat" without regard to the seating regulation at that time. This incident helps us recognize that 15 we have to devise a method of conveying historic events effectively to the next generation.

One solution to getting people without experiences such as the bus boycott movement to understand is by having them watch the movie *The Long Walk Home*. This movie effectively described how tough it was to continue with the 20 bus boycott movement for over one year. People without any experience would be deeply impressed to see people who kept walking on and on despite their exhaustion with the hope that the next generation wouldn't have the same terrible experience. They followed through with this movement in cooperation with one another by giving rides. It is Dr. King's distinguished leadership that 25 bound them together.

We can learn a lot from historic figures regarding how they fought to make society fair. We can tackle similar problems effectively by gaining clues in that movement.

Notes

l.4 **solidarity:** 団結 / l.6 **inspire:** ～を鼓舞する / l.7 **designated:** 指定されている / l.8 **regulation:** 規制 / l.9 **be arrested:** 逮捕される / l.11 **blatant segregation:** 露骨な差別待遇 / l.11 **courageous:** 勇敢な / l.12 **curator:** 学芸員 / l.16 **devise a method:** 方法を工夫する / l.16 **historic events:** 歴史上重要な出来事 / l.19 *The Long Walk Home*: ロング・ウォーク・ホーム（家路までの長い道程）、1990 年制作のアメリカ映画 / l.23 **exhaustion:** 極度の疲労 / l.24 **follow through with :** ～を最後までやり遂げる / l.26 **bind them together:** 彼らをまとめる / l.28 **clues:** ヒント

I. Reading Comprehension

Questions are based on the content of the text. Choose the best answer.

1. **How did people succeed with the noteworthy achievement?**
   (A) Through People's cooperation.
   (B) One person's political power did.
   (C) One author's literary work did.
   (D) The trends of the times did.

2. **What is Rose Parks famous for?**
   (A) She is famous for her distinguished leadership.
   (B) She is famous for her courageous action on a bus.
   (C) She is noted for raising women's status.
   (D) She is noted for her capabilities as a lawyer.

3. **How did the young African-American visitor react to the curator's question?**
   (A) She reacted emotionally to the question.
   (B) She gave a model answer to the question.
   (C) She replied without considering the era's background.
   (D) She gave her clearly defined reply to the question.

4. **What is one solution to getting people to understand without a similar experience?**
   (A) It is to encourage them to read books on history.
   (B) It is to have them listen to an expert's lecture on history.
   (C) It is to have them listen to famous quotes.
   (D) It is to have them vicariously experience it through a movie.

5. **How can we work on social problems?**
   (A) By finding clues in effective movements of the past.
   (B) By asking a person in authority to change the situation.
   (C) By acquiring the ability to think on our own.
   (D) By depending less on the people around us.

II. Sentence Completion

Nouns（名詞）

Choose the best answer as a synonym of the word(s) given in the bracket.

1. _____ led to remarkable achievements for people.　(Working together)

   (A) Solitude　　　　　　　　(B) Solution
   (C) Solidarity　　　　　　　(D) Solo

2. Rose Parks questioned the _____.　(official rule)

   (A) regularity　　　　　　　(B) regulation
   (C) register　　　　　　　　(D) region

3. African-Americans suffered openly from _____.　(unfair treatment)

   (A) segregation　　　　　　　(B) separation
   (C) sensation　　　　　　　　(D) sentiment

4. The question was : "If you were put in her _____, what would you do?"　(place)

   (A) status　　　　　　　　　(B) stature
   (C) possibility　　　　　　　(D) position

5. It is difficult to convey historic _____ to the next generation.　(important incidents)

   (A) events　　　　　　　　　(B) examples
   (C) essays　　　　　　　　　(D) estimates

日本語にすると同じ訳になる単語でも、文脈に応じて使い分けを！

たとえば「出来事」と日本語に訳される単語には、incidents と events がありますが、一般的な出来事には incidents、重要なあるいは特別な出来事には events と、文脈に応じて使い分ける必要があります。同様に、「歴史的な」と訳される語には、historical と historic がありますが、「歴史上で特に重要な出来事」を指す場合の形容詞には historic を用います。単語を覚えるときには、訳語だけでなく、ニュアンスも理解していきましょう。

III. Composition

Practice organizing your ideas based on what you have learned through reading. Remember that each person has different opinions and you have to give a detailed explanation.

1. What do you think about the African-American bus boycott movement?

   ex. I think it is amazing.

   [Points for improvement]
   Mention what is amazing and how it is amazing.

   [The revised answer]
   I am amazed at the fact that they continued with the movement for over one year. Their perseverance has touched me deeply.

   [Notes] perseverance: 忍耐力

   ....
   ....
   ....
   ....
   ....
   ....
   ....
   ....
   ....
   ....

2. What have you learned through reading about solidarity?

   ....
   ....
   ....
   ....
   ....
   ....
   ....
   ....
   ....
   ....

IV. Discussion

Practice expressing your opinions clearly. Have your own discussion using the sample below as a reference.

1. If you were put in the curator's place, how would you ask the visitor?

> **Sample discussion**
>
> **A:** If you were put in the curator's place, how would you ask the visitor?
> **B:** I would ask, "If you feel that a fundamental right is being violated, would you stand up for your right?"
> **A:** That's a good point because fundamental rights change depending on the situation.
> **B:** Right now, we can't do without a cellphone, so I may ask, "If your cellphone is taken away while you are abroad, would you stand up for your right?" How would you answer?
> **A:** That would depend on the situation. If fundamental rights concerning such an issue were not permitted in that country, I would adapt according to the local regulations.
>
> **[Notes]** stand up for your right: 権利を擁護する regulations: 規則

2. Do you have any experience making a remarkable achievement through solidarity? If your answer is yes, share your personal experience. If your answer is no, mention what you should have done in order to strengthen solidarity.

> ### 仮定法を用いた質問と相槌の打ち方
>
> ディスカッションで相手に質問する際は、
> **"If you were put in ... place, how would you ask?"**
> (〜の立場に立たされたら、どのように質問しますか)
> と仮定法を用いて相手に尋ねることで、議論をより深くすることができます。
> 相手の返答を評価する場合には、
> **"That's a good point."** (いいご指摘ですね)
> と相槌を打つことで、相手の発言をさらに促すことができるでしょう。また、"Yes" か "No" で返答ができない場合、depend on を使って、
> **"That would depend on the situation. / That depends on the situation."**
> (状況に拠るでしょう / 状況に拠ります)
> と言いながら意見をまとめて、議論を続けることができます。

Chapter 5

Technology's Contribution to Humanity (1)

日本に住んでいるときれいな水は容易に入手できますが、世界的に見ると稀であることにまず気付いてください。そして、科学技術の力を活用して、きれいな水をより多くの人々に提供できるように奮闘している人々がいることを認識しましょう。

Readings

As the exhibitions of The Tech Museum of Innovation in the State of California indicate, the progress of technology has benefited humanity. First of all, technology has contributed to our health. A photo of a girl who was drinking clean water and looked happy caught my eye. While it is hard to visualize the situation for Japanese people who are used to drinking safe tap 5 water, only 13 nations in the world are said to be able to drink tap water as it is. An American who often goes to developing countries for development assistance shared his experiences. "I help people in developing nations dig wells. Water from wells has improved the condition of their health. My family and friends ask, 'There are poor people here in the United States. Why don't 10 you help them?' However, I can help more people by assisting in developing nations. I once suffered from malaria, but even with that I refused to stop my activities."

The president of a Japanese company, Mr. Kanetoshi Oda contributed greatly to purifying water in a way different from digging wells. He 15 succeeded in transforming polluted water instantly into clean water by utilizing water purification tablets developed from fermented beans' bacteria. Anyone watching that demonstration with their own eyes would be deeply impressed by that magical power. As an additional measure against poverty, he established a system of selling water purification tablets at a low price by 20 employing local people.

Technology has also helped premature babies survive, physically challenged people walk with artificial legs, and has served to decrease the danger of surgery. A doctor who has performed surgery with robots mentioned the merits of the surgery. "Human beings have emotions and are swayed by 25 feelings each time. Robots, however, have no emotions, and operations by robots have increased the success rate."

However, there are many controversial issues regarding the progress of technology. Take the early detection of cancer, for instance. Some people can live longer because they have had surgery while others shorten their life 30 because they have undergone surgery. The latter type of people could have coexisted with cancer and lived out their natural life. Also, no one knows whether or not it is a wise decision to remove part of one's body beforehand due to the probability of cancer based on their genetic history. After taking the experts' opinions into consideration, we have to make the final decision on our 35 own responsibility.

Notes

l.1 **The Tech Museum of Innovation:** 科学革新博物館 / **l.5 tap water:** 水道水 / **l.8 dig wells:** 井戸を掘る / **l.15 purifying water:** 水の浄化 / **l.16 polluted water:** 汚染水 / **l.17 water purification tablets:** 水質浄化剤 / **l.17 fermented beans' bacteria:** 納豆菌 / **l.19 magical power:** 魔法のような力 / **l.22 premature babies:** 未熟児 / **l.22 physically challenged people:** 身障者 / **l.23 artificial legs:** 義足 / **l.25 surgery:** 外科手術 / **l.28 controversial:** 賛否両論別れる / **l.29 early detection:** 早期発見 / **l.34 probability:** 確率 / **l.34 genetic:** 遺伝学の / **l.35 on our own responsibility:** 自己責任で

I. Reading Comprehension

Questions are based on the content of the text. Choose the best answer.

1. How many people in the world can drink tap water as it is?
   (A) The majority of people do.
   (B) Two-thirds of people do.
   (C) Half of the population does.
   (D) Only a tiny number of people do.

2. How can the president of the Japanese company provide people in developing nations with clean water?
   (A) By helping people in developing nations dig wells.
   (B) By utilizing water purification tablets.
   (C) By developing infrastructure in developing nations.
   (D) By importing clean water from other countries.

3. What item is not mentioned as a contribution of technology?
   (A) To transmit traditional culture to the world.
   (B) To transform polluted water into clean water.
   (C) To raise premature babies successfully.
   (D) To assist physically challenged people in walking.

4. What is a true statement of surgery for potential cancer?
   (A) It is always a good policy to have an operation in advance.
   (B) It is an effective policy if patients believe in genetics.
   (C) There will be better policies as technology advances.
   (D) It is not necessarily a wise policy to have surgery beforehand.

5. How should we make the final decision?
   (A) We should decide without being affected by the experts' opinions.
   (B) We should decide without being influenced by the people around us.
   (C) We should decide after using the experts' opinions as a reference.
   (D) We should decide while valuing the experts' opinions.

II. Sentence Completion

Verbs（動詞）

Choose the best answer as a synonym of the word(s) given in the bracket.

1. Technology has _____ to our health. (made our health better)

   (A) contributed   (B) distributed

   (C) attributed   (D) retrieved

2. It is difficult for Japanese people to _____ the situation in developing countries. (picture)

   (A) violate   (B) videotape

   (C) victimize   (D) visualize

3. He has _____ polluted water by utilizing fermented beans' bacteria. (made it clean)

   (A) purified   (B) protected

   (C) proposed   (D) purchased

4. People can _____ surgery and live longer because of the early detection of cancer. (have)

   (A) undertake   (B) underestimate

   (C) underlie   (D) undergo

5. However, some people could have _____ their natural life without surgery. (survived)

   (A) lived for   (B) lived by

   (C) lived out   (D) lived on

---

live を使った２つの表現

"live out their natural life" は「天寿を全うする」という意味になります。例えば、「彼は延命治療を拒否し、105歳で天寿を全うされました」と言いたければ、
"He lived out his natural life until the age of 105 years old by declining prolonged treatment." となります。
併せて「（収入など）に頼って生きる」という意味の "live on" の使い方も確認しましょう。
"Temporary employees and part-timers don't have sufficient income to live on."
（派遣社員やアルバイトの人は十分な収入が得られません）

III. Composition

Practice organizing your ideas based on what you have learned through reading. Remember that each person has different opinions and you have to give a detailed explanation.

1. What have you learned through reading about water?

ex. I have learned that only 13 nations in the world can drink tap water as it is.

[Points for improvement]
Mention how the fact affects you.

[The revised answer]
I have learned that people who can drink clean tap water are in the minority on a global level and starting today, I will preserve as much water as possible.

2. What have you learned through reading about medicine?

IV. Discussion

Practice expressing your opinions clearly. Have your own discussion using the sample below as a reference.

1. **Would you consider going to a developing nation to help people there?**

> ### Sample discussion
>
> **A:** Would you consider going to a developing nation to help people there?
>
> **B:** Yes, I would like to help people in a developing nation while visualizing local people's happy faces by drinking clean water in the future.
>
> **A:** So would I. I have experience growing vegetables in my hometown. I would like to improve the skills further and teach local people how to grow vegetables effectively by using clean water.
>
> **B:** We can find great satisfaction doing that.
>
> **A:** A proverb says: "It's better to give than to receive."

2. **Japanese people in general have little concept of individual responsibility. What do you think people should decide to do on their own responsibility?**

> #### 自分自身の経験を語り、対話を深めましょう！
>
> 対話を深めるには、話題に関する自分自身の経験を語ることが有効です。例えば、Sample discussion では **"I have experience growing vegetables in my hometown."** と、自分の野菜を栽培した経験を語り、発展途上国の貢献には種々の形があることを示しています。
>
> そして、最後に諺 **"It's better to give than to receive."**（人に何かしてもらうより、人に何かしてあげる方がいい）と締め括っています。このように諺や決まり文句を使うことで対話から導き出したお互いの共通認識を一言でまとめることもできます。

Chapter 6 Technology's Contribution to Humanity (2)

日本人の発明が省エネや地球温暖化対策に役立っていることを理解しましょう。同時に、科学技術の発展の功罪も理解し、どの程度依存するのが妥当なのかについて検討してみましょう。

Readings

The exhibition of The Tech Museum of Innovation also deals with LED standing for light-emitting diode. Technology has provided people who didn't have electricity before with easy access to it. LED reminds us of the fact that three Japanese received the Nobel Prize in Physics for the invention of blue LED technology. The longevity of Blue LED is four times as great as 5 that of conventional electricity and its power consumption is one-tenth. It is energy-efficient and environmentally friendly, and is used in traffic lights and illuminations in public and in backlights of cellphones and TV in private. Besides saving electricity cost, it serves to save energy and as a measure against global warming. 10

A Japanese engineer visiting the museum lamented the situation in which Japanese engineers are put. "Many Japanese engineers go to the United States in order to continue with their research. This is also true of one of the Nobel Prize winners, Mr. Shuji Nakamura. While research requires a huge amount of money, engineers have difficulty raising funds." It has taken quite a while 15 since the issue of brain drain was pointed out, but no effective measures have been offered. It is an urgent issue that the government invests ample funds for promising projects without wasting tax revenue.

Moreover, the exhibition indicates that human rights activists have brought human rights abuses to light by making good use of security cameras. An 20 American visitor shared his experience. "In my community, security cameras have markedly decreased the crime rate." He added that discipline brought by Japanese companies to the United States is another factor for the decrease in the crime rate. Security cameras have produced efficacious results in Japan, too. It is often reported that the analysis of security cameras set up on streets have 25 identified criminals.

However, these same instruments have placed the movements of human rights activists under unwarranted surveillance by authoritarian regimes. This is not an issue that is limited only to human rights activists. This technology has also placed the actions of ordinary citizens under surveillance and 30 restricted their freedom. After weighing the positive and negative aspects of technology, we have to examine the appropriate degree to which we depend on technology.

Notes

l.1 LED = light-emitting diode: 発光ダイオード / **l.4 Physics:** 物理学 / **l.5 longevity:** 寿命 / **l.6 conventional:** 従来の / **l.6 power consumption:** 電力の消費 / **l.7 energy-efficient:** エネルギー効率がいい / **l.7 environmentally friendly:** 環境に優しい / **l.10 global warming:** 地球温暖化 / **l.11 lament:** ～を嘆く / **l.16 brain drain:** 頭脳流出 / **l.18 tax revenue:** 税収 / **l.19 human rights activists:** 人権活動家 / **l.21 security cameras:** 防犯カメラ / **l.22 discipline:** 規律 / **l.24 efficacious:** 効果のある / **l.28 unwarranted surveillance:** 不当な監視 / **l.28 authoritarian regimes:** 独裁政権

Exercises 6

I. Reading Comprehension

Questions are based on the content of the text. Choose the best answer.

1. What has made it possible for people in developing countries to get electricity?
   - (A) The use of water power generation.
   - (B) The use of LED technology.
   - (C) The utilization of nuclear power generation.
   - (D) The utilization of renewable energy.

2. How long does blue LED last compared with conventional electricity?
   - (A) It lasts one-tenth.
   - (B) It lasts for the same length.
   - (C) It lasts twice as long.
   - (D) It lasts four times as long.

3. How are blue LEDs used in public places?
   - (A) They are used in traffic lights.
   - (B) They are used in public lectures.
   - (C) They are utilized in cash registers.
   - (D) They are utilized in packing items.

4. How do human rights activists regard security cameras?
   - (A) They always regard the equipment positively.
   - (B) They regard the equipment more positively now than before.
   - (C) They rated the equipment more positively before than now.
   - (D) They are also aware of the negative aspects of security cameras.

5. How should we tackle technology in the future?
   - (A) We should depend more on technology than before.
   - (B) We should depend less on technology than before.
   - (C) We should carefully evaluate our dependence on technology.
   - (D) We shouldn't rely on technology at all.

II. Sentence Completion

Adjectives（形容詞）

Choose the best answer as a synonym of the word(s) given in the bracket.

1. Blue LED technology is _____ in terms of energy. (without a waste of energy)

   (A) efficient
   (B) eternal
   (C) enormous
   (D) eventful

2. Blu LED is _____ to the environment. (desirable)

   (A) keen
   (B) kind
   (C) friendly
   (D) frank

3. They served as a measure against _____ warming. (worldwide)

   (A) gross
   (B) grand
   (C) grateful
   (D) global

4. Research requires a _____ amount of money. (large)

   (A) huge
   (B) humble
   (C) handy
   (D) helpful

5. We need to weigh the _____ and negative aspects of technology. (favorable)

   (A) plus
   (B) positive
   (C) permanent
   (D) personal

物事のプラス面とマイナス面は、同時に考えましょう！

プラス面とマイナス面は、英語ではそれぞれ positive aspects と negative aspects と言います。大抵の物事には、プラスとマイナスの両面があるので、あなたの意見がプラス面に言及するものであれば敢えてマイナス面を、逆の場合は敢えてプラス面を考える習慣を身に付けておきましょう。そうすると物事を批判的に見る態度が養われ、自然と視野が広がっていきます。

III. Composition

Practice organizing your ideas based on what you have learned through reading. Remember that each person has different opinions and you have to give a detailed explanation.

1. **What have you learned through reading about blue LED technology?**

   ex. I have learned that it was invented by Japanese physicists.

   [Points for improvement]
   Mention what you think about the invention.

   [The revised answer]
   I have learned that it was invented by Japanese physicists, and I appreciate its cost performance concerning my telephone bill.

   ....
   ....
   ....
   ....
   ....
   ....
   ....
   ....
   ....
   ....

2. **What have you learned through reading about security cameras?**

   ....
   ....
   ....
   ....
   ....
   ....
   ....
   ....
   ....
   ....

IV. Discussion

Practice expressing your opinions clearly. Have your own discussion using the sample below as a reference.

1. If you were a politician, how would you spend research funds?

> **Sample discussion**
>
> **A:** If you were a politician, how would you spend research funds?
> **B:** I would spend the funds on the prediction of earthquakes.
> **A:** I was just about to say that. Earthquakes are predicted to hit Japan on a large scale in the near future.
> **B:** I think technological developments for accurate earthquake prediction are a worthwhile goal.
> **A:** I couldn't agree with you more. We earnestly hope for such developments.

2. Do you think more security cameras on streets should be set up in Japan?

同じ意見には同意を示し、議論を深めましょう！

Sample discussion のように、自分が言おうと思っていたことを相手が先に話題にした場合、**"I was just about to say that."**（私もそれを言おうとしていたのですよ）と言うことで、相手に同意を示し、話題をさらに発展させることができます。そして、相手の言ったことに 100% 同意する場合には、**"I couldn't agree with you more."**（全く同感です）を使い、**"We earnestly hope for ..."**（〜を切望しています）と続ければ、議論をより先に進めることができます。

Chapter 7

Coexistence of Computers and Humans

コンピューターが広く普及することで世界はどのように変化していったのでしょうか。その変遷を理解しましょう。そして、コンピューターが人間を潤す側面と、コンピューターの限界両面について考えてみましょう。

Readings

In the 19th century when the computer was invented, the development of computers for the general public was a gamble on whether or not it would pay off. Nobody could predict whether such a venture was wise or foolish. The Computer History Museum in the State of California has exhibitions on the history of computers over 2,000 years, from ancient times to the future from the perspective: "Computers change the world." Visitors can easily understand the transition of computers from abacuses to smartphones and AI.

At the present stage, computers benefit our life. In the future, however, no one can tell whether computers will continue to help us or take away our jobs. An exhibition on AI specifies: "We've long imagined machines able to replicate human thought and action. Computers provide the sophistication needed for human-like behavior."

In the same State of California, a fully automated restaurant opened ahead of other restaurants. The restaurant was very innovative. When customers order a dish they would like to have with their credit card, a machine reads the credit card, and projects the customer's name and the shelf number on a screen. Until customers receive the dish they have ordered, the only transactions they have is with machines. A businessperson who was waiting in a long line mentioned, "I often come here. Every restaurant is very crowded at lunchtime, and I have to wait long. Even when the line seems long at this restaurant, I can get my order quickly." The explanation says: Ingredients are selected by computer and healthy foods are used.

We have some concerns about how far AI will go, and when it goes to extremes, what humans should do. Robots that are considered to have human emotions have appeared. They take actions which suit the other person's words. In the near future, robots are predicted to be able to counsel patients suffering depression. However, a counselor who visited the above museum said flatly, "Counselors have to become aware of patients' ever-changing state of mind. Robots can't read such subtle psychology." We would like to believe that computers can just play a supplementary role for human beings.

Notes

l.7 **transition:** 変遷 / l.7 **abacuses:** そろばん / l.7 **AI (artificial intelligence):** 人工知能 / l.10 **replicate:** 〜を再現する / l.11 **sophistication:** 性能の高さ / l.14 **innovative:** 斬新な / l.17 **transactions:** やり取り / l.21 **ingredients:** 材料 / l.23 **go to extremes:** 極端に走る / l.27 **depression:** うつ病 / l.29 **subtle:** 微妙な / l.29 **psychology:** 心理 / l.30 **supplementary:** 補助的な

▌ Exercises 7 ▌

I. Reading Comprehension

Questions are based on the content of the text. Choose the best answer.

1. How did people in the 19th century regard computers?
   (A) They were certain that ordinary people would need computers soon.
   (B) They were doubtful whether ordinary people would need computers.
   (C) They thought that only some professionals could afford to buy computers.
   (D) They predicted that ordinary people wouldn't become interested in computers.

2. What is the focus of the Computer History Museum?
   (A) The focus is on artificial intelligence.
   (B) The focus is on smartphones.
   (C) The focus is on the historical aspects of computers.
   (D) The focus is on the prediction of future computers.

3. What will happen to us in the future?
   (A) Computers may not continue to benefit us.
   (B) We will depend less on computers.
   (C) We will depend more on computers.
   (D) Computers will certainly continue to benefit us.

4. Which job can't machines do at a fully automated restaurant?
   (A) To select foods that are healthy for customers.
   (B) To serve customers dishes that they order.
   (C) To reduce customers' waiting time.
   (D) To take a friendly attitude toward customers.

5. What is the present stage of robots?
   (A) Robots can only do mechanical jobs.
   (B) Robots can show emotions to some extent.
   (C) Robots can give helpful advice to patients.
   (D) Robots can understand subtle feelings.

II. Sentence Completion

Nouns（名詞）

Choose the best answer as a synonym of the word(s) given in the bracket.

1. In the 19th century no one could foresee if a _____ of mass-producing computers was wise. (trial)

   (A) benefit　　　　　　　(B) venture

   (C) version　　　　　　　(D) vision

2. The Computer History Museum deals with the _____ of computers. (change)

   (A) transition　　　　　　(B) transit

   (C) translation　　　　　(D) transaction

3. The museum looks at computers from a broader _____. (viewpoint)

   (A) perspective　　　　　(B) process

   (C) performance　　　　　(D) power

4. Customers at the restaurant have _____ with the machines. (dealings)

   (A) trainings　　　　　　(B) traits

   (C) transfers　　　　　　(D) transactions

5. Only human beings can read subtle _____. (the state of mind)

   (A) sychology　　　　　　(B) psychology

   (C) philosophy　　　　　(D) physiology

人の精神面に関する話題が多くなった現代

最近では、テレビや新聞、インターネットなどを通して人の精神面に着目した情報に触れることが増えました。たとえば、"Patients suffering depression are increasing because of continuous overwork."（残業が続いてうつ病患者が増えています）といった内容が報じられることも少なくありません。この英文で出てくる "depression"（憂鬱）や "overwork"（過労）など、日本語でもよく目にする語は、一度英語でどう言うのかを確認しておきましょう。また、日本語では "Illness starts in the mind."（病は気から）という諺がありますが、英語にも同様の表現があり、"It's all in your head."（気のせいだ）と言います。ちなみに、"psychology"（心理・心理学）は発音と綴りが異なるため、"p" を抜かすことが多くなりがちです。英語を書く時には、常に綴りにも注意しましょう。

III. Composition

Practice organizing your ideas based on what you have learned through reading. Remember that each person has different opinions and you have to give a detailed explanation.

1. What have you learned through reading about computers?

    ex. I have learned that the development of computers was once regarded as a gamble.

    [Points for improvement]
    Develop the idea.

    [The revised example]
    I have learned that it usually takes the general public a lot of time to accept innovation. We should take the long view of innovation.

    ....

    ....

    ....

    ....

    ....

    ....

    ....

    ....

    ....

2. Would you like to go to a fully automated restaurant?

    ....

    ....

    ....

    ....

    ....

    ....

    ....

    ....

    ....

    ....

IV. Discussion

Practice expressing your opinions clearly. Have your own discussion using the sample below as a reference.

1. In what way can we interpret human psychology that robots can't?

> **Sample discussion**
>
> **A:** In what way can we interpret human psychology that robots can't?
> **B:** In my case I usually pay special attention to the other person's facial expressions.
> **A:** I know facial expressions are more powerful than words.
> **B:** For instance, even when a friend said, "Fine, thank you" as a greeting, I can tell from her facial expressions that she had a bad day.
> **A:** We often have such experiences. I usually change the topic.
>
> [Notes] **She had a bad day:** その日彼女はついていなかった

2. What incident on computers or advertising is different from what you expected?

自分の意見を述べる時には、一言入れて話しましょう！

質問に対する応答が一つに限らないことを示したい場合、Sample discussion のように、**"In my case..."**（私の場合は ...）で始めましょう。
また、相手の発言内容を自分の言葉で言い換えて確認することで、相手の応答を熱心に聴いていることを示すことができます。
具体例をあげる際、**"For example"** がよく使われますが、それ以外に **"For instance"** も使われます。こちらも覚えて、実際に使えるようにしておきましょう。

Chapter 8 — Occupations AI can't Replace (1)

AI が人間の仕事を奪うと指摘されてから久しいですが、自分の職業は AI にはできないと言い切る人たちがいます。彼らは自分の職業をどのように捉え、働き甲斐を感じながら仕事をしているのでしょうか。

Readings

The previous units have dealt with how the United Nations and museums have worked on SDGs. Starting with this unit, the focus will be an individual person's active involvement in SDGs. While AI is expected to replace human beings in the workplace in the near future, some people declare that their occupations are stable. 5

First, let's listen to what a person working at an insurance company says. "My job requires human interaction, so I'm not worried about AI at all. AI can't replace me." He continued to say proudly, "No one can predict what will happen to themselves in rapidly changing times. Today's victor may be tomorrow's loser. A large number of Americans feel stressed, so I have come 10 up with a variety of products such as compensation for their absence from work, and provide these products for many companies." While he has found great satisfaction in his job, he has contributed to the revitalization of the economy.

Also, an American doctor mentioned fierce competition in the United States. "The United States is an extremely stressful society, and many people have mental and physical problems. Illness doesn't destroy human beings, but mental despair does destroy human beings. Through this career, I can learn a lot about the physical and mental aspects of human beings. I'm satisfied with it." He went on to say that the difference between doctors and clinical psychologists is that the former can use medication while the latter can't. He believed that medication is important for some patients.

On the other hand, a clinical psychologist mentioned. "I counsel teenagers suffering depression. They often have problems with their family because of their parents' discord and divorce. They can't get attention from their parents, so they are hungry for love. I advise them to go to church and take part in volunteer activities. Through their activities, they have become aware that some people are worse off than themselves, and are willing to work on volunteer activities. When I see them developing a positive attitude, it makes me feel it's all worthwhile."

The rapidly growing demand for doctors and clinical psychologists has revitalized the economy. It is hard to regard that reality as 100% desirable, but it is an unquestionable fact that AI can't replace doctors and clinical psychologists.

Notes

l.5 **stable:** 安泰な / l.6 **insurance company:** 保険会社 / l.11 **compensation:** 補償 / l.13 **revitalization of the economy:** 経済の活性化 / l.15 **fierce competition:** 過当競争 / l.17 **destroy:** 〜を滅ぼす / l.18 **despair:** 絶望 / l.20 **clinical psychologists:** 臨床心理学者 / l.21 **the former:** 前者 / l.21 **medication:** 薬の投与 / l.21 **the latter:** 後者 / l.25 **discord:** 不和 / l.30 **worthwhile:** 価値のある

Exercises 8

I. Reading Comprehension

Questions are based on the content of the text. Choose the best answer.

1. How will the role of AI be regarded in the near future?
   - (A) AI will play a bigger role.
   - (B) The role of AI will remain unchanged.
   - (C) AI will play a minor role.
   - (D) AI will be regarded as out-of-date.

2. What does the person working at an insurance company think about his future?
   - (A) He is very concerned about it because he may lose his job.
   - (B) He is a little worried about it because no one can predict the future.
   - (C) He is confident about his prospects because AI can't take away his job.
   - (D) He is indifferent to it because his main concern is the present.

3. What is the difference between doctors and clinical psychologists?
   - (A) Doctors can prescribe medicine, but clinical psychologists can't.
   - (B) While doctors believe in the effect of medicine, clinical psychologists don't.
   - (C) Although clinical psychologists treat patients suffering from depression, doctors don't.
   - (D) Only clinical psychologists, not doctors, focus on the mental aspects of human beings.

4. What advice does the clinical psychologist give to teenagers suffering from depression?
   - (A) Help your mother with the housework because she is busy with her outside work.
   - (B) Have a part-time job in order to support your mother financially.
   - (C) Take care of your younger brothers and sisters because they need supervision.
   - (D) Participate in volunteer activities so that you can broaden your views.

5. Will doctors and clinical psychologists continue to be in demand in the future?
   - (A) It will be a marked increase.
   - (B) It will be a gradual increase.
   - (C) It will remain unchanged.
   - (D) It will be a sharp decrease.

II. Sentence Completion

Adjectives（形容詞）

Choose the best answer as a synonym of the word(s) given in the bracket.

1. Some people's occupations are _____. (steady)

    (A) special   (B) stable
    (C) still   (D) staple

2. A large number of Americans feel _____. (stressed)

    (A) stressful   (B) stress
    (C) strange   (D) strategic

3. The doctor mentioned _____ competition in the United States. (very strong)

    (A) final   (B) fabulous
    (C) furious   (D) fierce

4. The doctor is _____ with his profession. (pleased)

    (A) content   (B) satisfied
    (C) fond   (D) glad

5. He can learn a lot about the physical and _____ aspects of human beings. (spiritual)

    (A) medal   (B) manual
    (C) mental   (D) mammal

単語を覚える時は、ニュアンスの確認を！

"be satisfied with" と "be content with" は、どちらも「〜に満足している」と訳しますが、同じ意味ではありません。"be content with" は「（一応）満足している」という意味となり、"I'm content with my job." と言えば、「（総合的に見ると、一応自分の仕事に）満足している」という旨を表します。英単語を覚える時には、出来る限り英英辞典などを引いて定義と用例を確認し、言外の意味もつかみましょう。

III. Composition

Practice organizing your ideas based on what you have learned through reading. Remember that each person has different opinions and you have to give a detailed explanation.

1. **What do you think about the statement: "Today's winner may be tomorrow's loser"?**

   ex. I think this applies especially to the business world. I have seen many examples around me.

   [Points for improvement]
   Mention what specific examples you have seen.

   [The revised answer]
   I think this applies especially to the business world. In my hometown many shops were once busy with a lot of local customers. However, large-scale supermarkets have replaced these shops. I have seen many shops close one after another.

   ....

   ....

   ....

   ....

   ....

   ....

   ....

   ....

   ....

2. **What do you try to do in order to ease your stress?**

   ....

   ....

   ....

   ....

   ....

   ....

   ....

   ....

   ....

IV. Discussion

Practice expressing your opinions clearly. Have your own discussion using the sample below as a reference.

1. **What do you think about competition?**

> ### Sample discussion
>
> **A:** What do you think about competition?
> **B:** I think it's necessary. Through my club activity of baseball, I have realized that competition is necessary.
> **A:** Can you tell me more about that?
> **B:** Through competition we have become highly motivated to practice harder.
> **A:** You must have improved your baseball skills effectively.
>
> **[Notes] improve your baseball skills:** 野球の技術を磨く （**skill up** は和製英語）

2. **What values about occupations have you found through your personal experiences or indirect experiences such as through books and movies?**

> ### 相手の経験についての発言を促したい場合
>
> 相手の経験についてさらに聴きたい場合は、Sample discussion のように相手によって表現を使い分けましょう。
>
> 友達など親しい人の場合
> **"Can you tell me more about that?"** （もっと詳しく話してもらえますか）
>
> 目上の人の場合
> **"Would you tell me more about that?"** （もっと詳しく話して頂けますか）
> そして発言を聴いた後に **"You must have improved your baseball skills effectively."** （きっと効率よく技術を磨かれたことでしょうね）と相手を立てるコメントをすると会話が続き易くなるでしょう。

Chapter 9 | *Occupations AI can't Replace (2)*

自分の仕事に生き甲斐を見出している人は、保険会社や医療従事者だけに限定されません。投資銀行や接客業に携わっている人の中にも、職場で経験する不都合な出来事を巧みに処理することによって、やり甲斐を実感し続けながら、経済成長に貢献していることを学びましょう。

Readings

Occupations that AI can't replace are not limited to insurance companies and the medical profession. Employees in investment banks and the hospitality industry are also secure. They calmly cope with problems they face in their workplace or actively acquire skills required in their workplace without being complacent with their stable condition. Through these active endeavors, they 5 produce favorable results and contribute to economic development.

An American working at an investment bank shared his experiences. "Stocks go up and down rapidly, and things don't necessarily work out as expected. Clients sometimes take their frustration out on me. In such cases, I explain in detail that I have paid meticulous attention, but something 10

50

unexpected has happened." And he tells himself that it is the same when he introduces a friend to a first-rate restaurant, and even if the friend accidentally suffers from food poisoning, he doesn't have to take responsibility for the food poisoning.

Also, a Hispanic-American working in the hospitality industry mentioned how he should treat Caucasian-Americans. "Some Caucasian-Americans speak in a condescending tone. Every time I encounter such customers, I recall my mother's words: There are some nasty people anywhere. Don't waste your energy on such people." I try to stay professional and disregard those people's unpleasant attitudes.

Furthermore, a Japanese-American shared his experience. "A lot of Japanese-Americans are modest. Modesty is regarded as a virtue in Japanese culture, but on Wall Street modest people are taken advantage of. In the business world it is indispensable to promote ourselves by emphasizing our strong points and achievements. This agrees with the remarks of an introverted Caucasian-American. "I'm introverted by nature, but I have altered my attitude through training. While we can't readily change our personality, we can adjust our attitude to meet the demands necessary for the situation." She told me that she took some courses on speeches, got used to speaking in public through repeated practices, and learned to express her opinions with confidence. Now she can speak comfortably with anyone.

The statements of the above people are filled with clues on how to avoid misfortune and invite happiness to us. How we interpret our daily experiences and how we change our approach to life determine whether we can make our life brighter or darker. We need to contemplate words of wisdom from people who have succeeded in creating a happier life for themselves.

Notes

l.2 **the medical profession:** 医療従事者 / l.2 **investment banks:** 投資銀行 / l.2 **the hospitality industry:** 接客業 / l.5 **complacent with their stable condition:** 安定した状態にあぐらをかく / l.5 **endeavors:** 努力 / l.9 **take their frustration out on:** 〜に八つ当たりする / l.10 **meticulous:** 細心の / l.15 **Hispanic-American:** ヒスパニック系アメリカ人（祖先がスペイン語を母国語とするラテンアメリカ系の人）/ l.17 **condescending tone:** 上から目線の口調 / l.18 **nasty:** 不快な / l.19 **disregard:** 〜を無視する / l.22 **virtue:** 美徳 / l.23 **be taken advantage of:** 利用される / l.24 **indispensable:** 不可欠な / l.24 **promote ourselves:** 自己PRする / l.25 **introverted:** 内向的な / l.35 **contemplate:** 〜を熟考する / l.35 **words of wisdom:** 金言

I. Reading Comprehension

Questions are based on the content of the text. Choose the best answer.

1. What does the investment bank clerk do when something unexpected happens?
   (A) He apologizes to his clients many times.
   (B) He compensates his clients for their losses.
   (C) He tries to convince his clients by fast-talking them.
   (D) He gives detailed explanations of the incident.

2. What is the point of the Hispanic-American mother's words?
   (A) Acquire polite expressions necessary in the hospitality industry.
   (B) Alter your communication styles to others.
   (C) Don't pay attention to nasty people.
   (D) Save your energy through exercise.

3. What is an accurate description of the Japanese-American on Wall Street?
   (A) He cherishes the Japanese value of modesty.
   (B) He transmits traditional Japanese values to Americans.
   (C) He helps newcomers get used to their life on Wall Street.
   (D) He modifies his attitude so that he isn't taken advantage of.

4. What did the introverted European-American do in order to reform herself?
   (A) She practiced giving speeches in public over and over again.
   (B) She listened attentively to famous speeches in the United States.
   (C) She took notes of novel ideas that occurred to her.
   (D) She read a lot of how-to books in the library.

5. What can we learn from the characters appearing in this chapter?
   (A) How to decide what products we should invest in.
   (B) How to hand down our traditional values to the next generation.
   (C) How to deal with unpleasant experiences in our daily life.
   (D) How to show respect for different ethnic groups.

II. Sentence Completion

Verbs（動詞）

Choose the best answer as a synonym of the word(s) given in the bracket.

1. Whenever he _____ nasty customers, he recalls his mother's words.
   (happens to meet)

   (A) embraces   (B) encounters
   (C) embarrasses   (D) enforces

2. A Japanese-American _____ his experience. (mentioned)

   (A) told   (B) said
   (C) shared   (D) gave

3. In the business world it is indispensable to _____ ourselves. (sell our abilities)

   (A) appeal   (B) do
   (C) progress   (D) promote

4. Businesspeople have to _____ their opinions with confidence. (state)

   (A) express   (B) tell
   (C) say   (D) get

5. We need to _____ words of wisdom. (consider)

   (A) construct   (B) contemplate
   (C) console   (D) conduct

自己 PR は具体的に！

本文で出てきたように、「自己 PR する」や「アピールする」は、直訳の "do PR" や "appeal oneself" ではなく、**"promote oneself"** と言います。

自己 PR する際は、「○○するのが好きです」や「○○するのを楽しんでいます」と言うと相手にあまり響かないので、例えば、

"I'm friendly to anyone, so I can treat even difficult customers tactfully."
（誰にでも友好的なので、気むずかしいお客さんでもうまく対応できます）

"I'm meticulous, so I can treat each customer in a way that I can meet the customer's needs."
（几帳面なので、お客さんのニーズに合わせた対応ができます）

といったように具体的に何が出来るのかを伝えると、自分の強みを相手に印象づけることができるでしょう。

III. Composition

Practice organizing your ideas based on what you have learned through reading. Remember that each person has different opinions and you have to give a detailed explanation.

1. Recall one incident that you can interpret differently.

   ex. When I was working part-time at a restaurant, we had many customers. Some employees were irritated while others were happy.

   [Points for improvement]
   Give the reason in each case.

   [The revised answer]
   When I was working part-time at a restaurant, we had many customers. Some employees were irritated with the workload while others were happy with the popularity of the restaurant attracting good business.

2. Have you changed your attitude through training? If your answer is yes, share your experiences. If your answer is no, recall one attitude of yours and mention how you could have improved it through training.

IV. Discussion

Practice expressing your opinions clearly. Have your own discussion using the sample below as a reference.

1. When you come across customers complaining about a service or product in your workplace, how should you deal with those customers?

> ### Sample discussion
>
> **A:** How do you deal with problem complainers in your workplace?
> **B:** They often hope that someone will listen to their complaints.
> **A:** Do you still listen to what they say even when it is their fault?
> **B:** Yes, I have learned through my experiences to listen attentively to their complaints without interrupting them. Then, they usually calm down.
> **A:** Thank you for your practical advice. Starting next time, I'll follow your example.
>
> **[Notes] problem complainers:** クレーマー（クレーマーは和製英語）/ **listen to what they say:** 彼らの話に耳を傾ける / **calm down:** 落ち着く / **follow your example:** あなたを見習う

2. How would you promote yourself so that Americans won't regard you as incapable?

相手の発言について疑問をもった場合

相手の発言に納得いかなかった場合、頭ごなしに相手の発言を否定せずに、疑問に焦点を当てて質問しましょう。Sample discussion のように、
"Do you still listen to what they say even when it is their fault?"
（相手に非がある場合でも、相手の話に耳を傾けるのですか）
と質問しましょう。例のように、相手の質問の答えが効果的だと思ったら、
"Starting next time, I'll follow your example."
（次回から、あなたを見習います）
と続けましょう。

Chapter 10
Utilizing an Indomitable Spirit

ウォール街において女性やマイノリティが成功を収めるには、多大な困難が伴います。しかし、少数派ながら実際に成功を手中にした人々もいます。彼らが、個人的にどのような努力をして不平等を乗り越えたのか苦心談に耳を傾けましょう。

Readings

It is difficult for anyone to achieve success on Wall Street. Nevertheless, there are successful minorities and women who are exceptions. When I interviewed those people, I found out that they displayed an indomitable spirit. In order to be successful, they had made superhuman efforts that ordinary people could never imagine. 5

A: "I was brought up in a poor village in Jamaica. In my childhood I used to envy other children, 'That child wears new clothes' and 'That child wears shoes.' However, a certain man suggested I go to a hospital. In that hospital, I saw people who were faced with death because of terminal cancer and who were just waiting for an organ transplant. 10

While looking at those people, I reformed myself, 'I'm blessed with health. What should I complain about?' That experience made me change my philosophy."

Since then, he has had a better opinion of his life, and has made up his mind to forge his course in life. By studying very hard, he won a scholarship 15 to a university in the United States. Today he is active on the front line of Wall Street.

The next character is a woman who is rare on Wall Street.

B: "Almost all people working on Wall Street are men. Unless women make by far greater efforts than men, women won't be recognized. 20 Fortunately, I have been recognized as professionally competent, and I work as a strategic adviser at a bank. When a company would like to acquire another company, I work as a mediator or give some advice to the company we have conducted business transactions with. I need to read and analyze a huge amount of data before making a final decision." 25

She mentioned that her success arises from her diligence and personality. Acquiring companies is a complicated task, and her colleagues feel stressed. However, she finds satisfaction working out strategies. Even when her negotiations haven't worked well, she can explore the cause of failure without feeling frustrated and draw lessons from that experience. 30

One characteristic that the above people have in common is their strong willpower which has turned disadvantageous situations to their advantage. The man has joined the circle of successful people by overcoming his poverty in his childhood, and the woman has worked on a par with men by getting over gender discrimination on Wall Street. Their messages inspire people who 35 would like to achieve success anywhere, not just on Wall Street.

Notes

l.3 **indomitable spirit:** 不屈の精神 / l.4 **superhuman efforts:** 桁外れの努力 / l.10 **terminal cancer:** 末期がん / l.10 **organ transplant:** 臓器移植 / l.11 **reform myself:** 改心する / l.13 **philosophy:** 人生観 / l.15 **forge his course in life:** 進路を切り拓く / l.16 **front line:** 第一線 / l.18 **character:** 登場人物 / l.22 **strategic adviser:** 戦略的助言者 / l.23 **acquire:** ～を買収する / l.23 **mediator:** 仲介者 / l.27 **colleagues:** 同僚 / l.34 **on a par:** 互角に / l.35 **gender discrimination:** 性差別

Exercises 10

I. Reading Comprehension

Questions are based on the content of the text. Choose the best answer.

1. What was the Jamaican man's childhood like?

   (A) He was happy because he was blessed with nature.

   (B) He was happy because he led a spiritually rich life.

   (C) He was unhappy because he contrasted his material life with others.

   (D) He was unhappy because he suffered from a serious illness.

2. What made the above Jamaican man change his philosophy?

   (A) Exposing himself to nature did.

   (B) Reading an inspiring book did.

   (C) Suffering from a serious illness did.

   (D) Visiting a local hospital did.

3. What is reality like on Wall Street?

   (A) More women are active than men.

   (B) Gender equality has already been achieved.

   (C) Men and women are almost equal.

   (D) There is still a long way to go to achieve gender equality.

4. What is the woman's task?

   (A) She gives advice to companies that hope to start a business.

   (B) She gives advice to companies that hope to expand their business.

   (C) She offers advice to individuals who hope to invest in stocks.

   (D) She offers advice to individuals who hope to expand their investments.

5. What is the above woman's personality like?

   (A) She is optimistic.

   (B) She is pessimistic.

   (C) She is cautious.

   (D) She is friendly to everyone.

II. Sentence Completion

Collocations（言葉の組み合わせ）

Choose the best answer as a synonym of the word(s) given in the bracket.

1. Some people have _____ on Wall Street despite the fierce competition. (succeeded)

   (A) achieved success   (B) got success

   (C) done success   (D) made success

2. The man _____ by looking at the patients in the local hospital. (positively changed his philosophy)

   (A) remodeled himself   (B) reexamined himself

   (C) reformed himself   (D) regained himself

3. He became aware that he shouldn't _____ about his life because he is blessed with health. (complain)

   (A) voice complaints   (B) say complaints

   (C) voice claims   (D) say claims

4. The woman has to _____ after a complicated analysis. (decide)

   (A) do a decision   (B) make a decision

   (C) get a decision   (D) take a decision

5. It is important to _____ from experiences. (learn)

   (A) get lessons   (B) take lessons

   (C) draw lessons   (D) make lessons

和製英語に注意

「リフォーム」という言葉は、英語ではニュアンスが異なります。たとえば、"reform oneself" で「改心する」という意味になり、**"He reformed himself by visiting patients in the local hospital."**（彼は地方の病院の患者を見舞ったことによって改心しました）のように用います。また、「～を改革する」という意味もあり、**"The educational policy in Japan should be reformed so that students can develop their own distinctive personalities and abilities."**（日本の教育制度は、学生自身の個性や能力が伸ばせるように改革されるべきです）のように用います。ちなみに「家をリフォームする」という場合は、**"remodel a house"** となり reform は使われないので、注意しましょう。

III. Composition

Practice organizing your ideas based on what you have learned through reading. Remember that each person has different opinions and you have to give a detailed explanation.

1. Think about efforts to overcome economic disparity. Count your blessings instead of voicing complaints.

   ex. I have to work part-time and I once envied some classmates who didn't have to work part-time. However, I have begun to think that I have gained something through my part-time job.

   [Points for improvement]
   Mention specifically what you have benefited from your part-time job.

   [The revised answer]
   I have to work part-time and I once envied some classmates who didn't have to work part-time. However, I have had a better opinion of my part-time job: I have acquired skills in how to treat customers politely through my part-time job.

   [Notes] economic disparity: 経済格差

   ....
   ....
   ....
   ....
   ....
   ....
   ....

2. Recall one incident where you voiced complaints, and think about how you could have counted your blessings in that incident.

   ....
   ....
   ....
   ....
   ....
   ....
   ....

IV. Discussion

Practice expressing your opinions clearly. Have your own discussion using the sample below as a reference.

1. Give a successful example of a person who overcame economic disparity. If you can't think of any person, search for information on the Internet.

> ### Sample discussion
>
> **A:** Have you ever heard of a successful example of a person who overcame economic disparity?
>
> **B:** Yes, one example is the past Prime Minister in Japan, Kakuei Tanaka.
>
> **A:** I've heard of the name before, but I don't know much about him. Can you explain in more detail about his success story?
>
> **B:** He was a graduate of elementary school, accepted life's challenges and climbed to the top of the political ladder.
>
> **A:** That's terrific! His success story can inspire us.
>
> **[Notes]** terrific: 素晴らしい   inspire us: 私達を鼓舞してくれる

2. Give a successful example of a person who overcame racial discrimination or gender discrimination. If you can't recall any person, search for information on the Internet.

話題に詳しくない時は、積極的に尋ねましょう！

自分のあまり詳しくない話題が話されている時は、何を知りたいのかを明確にして、積極的に質問することが大切です。

友達など親しい人の場合

"Can you explain in more detail about ...?"
(～について詳しく説明してもらえますか)

目上の人の場合

"Would you explain in more detail about...?"
(～について詳しく説明して頂けますか)

詳しく説明してもらった後は、"good" のような普段からよく使っている表現は避けて、**"terrific!"**（素晴らしい）などの形容詞を使って感想を述べる方が望ましいでしょう。

Chapter 11 | *The Positive Influence of Martial Arts*

柔道の創始者・嘉納治五郎の「自他共栄」の精神は、柔道だけではなく、多方面にわたって活かされていることを読み取りましょう。そして、目標を達成するには、他者との協力が不可欠なので、お互いが潤う道を選択することの重要性を認識しましょう。

Readings

Famous words by Jigoro Kano who is called the father of judo are: "Overcome yourself rather than beat others." Let's listen to how some Americans overcame personal challenges by learning martial arts.

One American shared his experience as follows: "My family was poor. My parents didn't care about me because all they had time to do was work. I felt 5 lonely and got mixed up with bad company. My parents learned that I had been hanging out with bad company and made me learn martial arts." He told me that he threw himself into judo later and broke off his relationship with bad company.

The second American said, "I was a delicate child, and my parents 10

62

suggested I learn judo." At first he wasn't enthusiastic about judo. However, he made a decision after learning about the originator of judo, Jigoro Kano's way of life. While Jigoro Kano was short and at a physical disadvantage, he thought out ways to win by turning his opponent's power to his own advantage and became an expert in that field. 15

The third American stated, "Americans in general are obsessed with freedom. I have trained both my body and mind through martial arts and have acquired self-control. It is essential to make freedom and discipline compatible." He continued to share his experience. "I can apply what I have learned through martial arts to business. First, I can control my emotions and devote myself 20 toward my goals. I have acquired the habit of looking at the situation from a broader perspective. My way of conducting business is just one way, and I can figure out that the other party has an alternative in mind. I can see the other party's intent, so I can come up with solutions which can convince the other party." Besides that, he mentioned an anecdote about Jigoro Kano which 25 moved spectators. Jigoro Kano extended a helping hand to his opponent so as to avoid an injury to the head when throwing his opponent to the floor. By the influence from Jigoro Kano, he has been careful not to damage the other party in business. While taking notice that human beings are apt to be swayed by emotions and be blinded by immediate benefits, he tries to explore rational 30 solutions which benefit both parties.

These three people have different results, but they have martial arts in common. It is worth noting that martial arts serve to teach discipline and fair play overcoming personal weaknesses.

Notes

martial arts: 武道 / **l.3 personal challenges:** 個人的な難題 / **l.6 get mixed up with:** (危険な仲間) と付き合う / **l.7 bad company:** 不良仲間 / **l.8 throw himself into:** 〜に夢中になる / **l.8 break off:** (人間関係) を絶つ / **l.12 originator:** 創始者 / **l.14 turn his opponent's power to his own advantage:** 対戦相手の力を利用する / **l.16 be obsessed with:** 〜にとらわれる / **l.18 make ... compatible:** 〜を両立させる / **l.20 devote myself:** 専念する / **l.22 perspective:** 観点 / **l.24 convince:** 〜を納得させる / **l.25 anecdote:** 逸話 / **l.26 spectators:** 観客 / **l.30 explore:** 〜を模索する / **l.30 rational:** 理にかなった / **l.31 benefit:** 〜を潤す / **l.33 fair play:** 正々堂々とした振る舞い

Exercises 11

I. Reading Comprehension

Questions are based on the content of the text. Choose the best answer.

1. Why did the first American get mixed up with bad company?
    (A) Both he and fellow members were interested in martial arts.
    (B) Fellow members showed sympathy toward his environment.
    (C) His parents weren't concerned about him because of their tight schedule.
    (D) His parents interfered too much in his private matters.

2. What made the second American learn judo?
    (A) His elementary school teacher urged him to learn judo.
    (B) His parents encouraged him to learn judo.
    (C) He wanted to get over his inferiority complex of being short.
    (D) He decided to overcome his inferiority complex of being a delicate child.

3. What is an accurate description of the third American?
    (A) He believed that he should pursue freedom throughout his whole life.
    (B) He believed that freedom should be given priority in the United States.
    (C) He thought that discipline is more important than freedom.
    (D) He thought that striking a balance between freedom and discipline is important.

4. What habit did the above American acquire through martial arts?
    (A) Viewing the situation from a different perspective.
    (B) Paying attention to immediate benefits.
    (C) Analyzing similar past incidents.
    (D) Showing only positive emotions effectively.

5. What type of performance by Jigoro Kano touched the spectators?
    (A) His speedy and powerful performance did.
    (B) The effective use of his skills did.
    (C) His consideration for his opponent's safety did.
    (D) His enthusiasm toward judo did.

II. Sentence Completion

Nouns（名詞）

Choose the best answer as a synonym of the word(s) given in the bracket.

1. The American got mixed up with bad _____. (fellow members)

   (A) company
   (B) colleague
   (C) co-worker
   (D) content

2. He put the _____ with those people to an end later. (association)

   (A) relative
   (B) relationship
   (C) reliance
   (D) relevance

3. The businessperson has trained both his body and _____. (mental aspect)

   (A) soul
   (B) spirit
   (C) mind
   (D) muscle

4. He believed that _____ is also important. (controlling oneself)

   (A) decision
   (B) discipline
   (C) diligence
   (D) dignity

5. Jigoro Kano moved his spectators by his consideration for the _____. (rival in a game)

   (A) colleague
   (B) companion
   (C) enemy
   (D) opponent

語彙学習の際は、辞書を引くことを忘れずに！

"company" の訳語は「会社」とだけ覚えていることが多いかもしれませんが、上記のように "bad company" で「不良仲間」という意味にも用いられます。また、"good company" で「話していて楽しい仲間（相手）」、人と話して楽しかった時に、**"You've been good company."** あるいは **"I've enjoyed your company"**（お話して楽しかったです）と別れ際に言うこともできます。新しい単語に触れたら必ず辞書を引き、複数の意味と例文にも目を通しておく習慣を身に付けましょう。

III. Composition

Practice organizing your ideas based on what you have learned through reading. Remember that each person has different opinions and you have to give a detailed explanation.

1. **Think about how you have compensated for some items which seem to be weak points.**

   ex. I belong to a baseball club. I'm slim which seems to be a weak point because I'm not a powerful hitter. However, I'm still active in games.

   [Points for improvement]
   Describe specifically how you're active in games.

   [The revised answer]
   I belong to a baseball club. I'm slim which seems to be a weak point because I'm not a powerful hitter. However, I have contributed to my team by being a skilled fielder.

   ....
   ....
   ....
   ....
   ....
   ....
   ....
   ....
   ....

2. **Think about how your teammate or someone you know could compensate for some items which seemed to be weak points.**

   ....
   ....
   ....
   ....
   ....
   ....
   ....
   ....
   ....

IV. Discussion

Practice expressing your opinions clearly. Have your own discussion using the sample below as a reference.

1. How can you apply what you have acquired through sports to your study?

> **Sample discussion**
>
> **A:** How have you applied what you have acquired through sports to your study?
>
> **B:** I have applied my power of concentration acquired through track and field to English learning.
>
> **A:** When learning English, how have you made good use of your power of concentration?
>
> **B:** I have memorized many English words by utilizing my power of concentration while waiting for a train.
>
> **A:** You have acquired a good habit, haven't you?
>
> **[Notes]** power of concentration: 集中力

2. How can you apply what you have acquired through sports to your workplace?

相手の発言に種々の解釈が成り立つ場合

相手の発言を聞き返す際、**"Would you say that again? "**（もう一度言って頂けますか）と言う場合が多いですが、この表現では自分がどこまで理解できているのか伝えることはできません。聞き返す際は、理解した点と何を聞きたいのかを明確にして、
"When learning English, how have you made good use of your power of concentration? "（英語を学習する際、どのように集中力を活用しているのですか）などと、焦点を絞って質問することが必要です。そして、相手のさらなる発言を聴いた際、ただ聞き流すのではなく、必ず感想を述べましょう。

Chapter 12 — Japanese Anime's Contribution to the Global Community

日本のアニメに啓発されたアメリカ人が、自然との共存の大切さを認識し、地球温暖化の防止に貢献したいと考えるようになった経緯を読み取りましょう。また、善悪の間に明確な境界線を引くことの危険性にも気付き、民族間の対立を避け、協力して目標を達成することの重要性もつかみましょう。

Readings

Like martial arts, Japanese anime has exerted a considerable influence on young Americans. It has given them an educational opportunity to reconsider their preconceptions.

A young American who became motivated to learn Japanese by watching anime spoke to me. "What cultural values do Japanese people cherish?" I replied, "Traditionally we firmly believe that we should coexist harmoniously with nature. Many Western people believe that they can conquer nature, but the idea of conquering nature is arrogant." He chimed in, "Recently a lot of Americans have become aware of that. Large-scale wildfires which have never been imagined before have frequently taken place. However, no

68

effective measures to put out wildfires have been taken." He told me that he is concerned with environmental issues and is applying himself to developing environmentally friendly energy resources.

As for another difference in values between Japanese and Western people, I mentioned, "Traditionally Japanese people don't think it's possible to draw a clear line between good and evil while many Western people seem to think they can clearly distinguish good from evil based on dualism." He then shared his experience with me. "By watching Japanese anime, I have been affected by Japanese philosophy and I have been able to view tragic incidents in the world from a different perspective. For example, I shouldn't assume that people who abuse minority groups are evil. Evil ideas are imprinted on their mind, but I have begun to wonder if we can help them change their ways of thinking through dialog and education." When I commented, "You have positive thinking," he replied, "I was a negative thinker by nature, but I have experienced positive influences through Japanese anime."

Japanese people have neglected to transmit traditional Japanese ways of thinking to other countries. Recently however, anime has played that role. The main cause of conflicts lies in the fact that the people concerned assume themselves to be absolutely right and the other party to be absolutely wrong. Unless they listen to what the other side has to say and find a middle ground, they will have endless conflicts. If young Americans who have had an educational influence from Japanese anime start to coexist with nature and then aim at reconciling with other ethnic groups, they can transform the world into a comfortable place to live in. And if Japanese people continue to share the traditional ways of thinking with other nations, that can be a significant contribution to the global community.

Notes

l.3 preconceptions: 先入観 / l.6 coexist harmoniously with nature: 自然と調和して共存する / l.7 conquer: ～を征服する / l.8 arrogant: 傲慢な / l.8 chime in: 相槌を打つ / l.9 wildfires: 山火事 / l.13 energy resources: エネルギー源 / l.17 distinguish: ～を区別する / l.17 dualism: 二元論 / l.19 tragic incidents: 悲惨な出来事 / l.20 assume: ～と決めつける / l.21 abuse: ～を虐待する / l.26 transmit: ～を発信する / l.30 middle ground: 妥協点 / l.33 reconcile with: ～と和解する / l.35 significant contribution: 重要な貢献

Exercises 12

I. Reading Comprehension

Questions are based on the content of the text. Choose the best answer.

1. **What made the young American learn Japanese?**
   (A) His parents' recommendation did.
   (B) A suggestion from his close friend did.
   (C) Experiences watching Japanese anime did.
   (D) Experiences visiting sightseeing spots in Japan did.

2. **What have many Western people recognized recently?**
   (A) People can easily conquer nature with technology.
   (B) People should explore different ways to conquer nature.
   (C) People can certainly conquer nature in the near future.
   (D) People shouldn't attempt to conquer nature.

3. **What is an accurate description of Japanese and Western people?**
   (A) Many Western people think they can tell the difference between good and evil while Japanese people don't.
   (B) Many Japanese think they can tell the difference between good and evil while Western people don't.
   (C) Both Western and Japanese people think they can distinguish between good and evil.
   (D) Neither Western nor Japanese people think they can distinguish between good and evil.

4. **What is true of the young American's personality?**
   (A) He is a positive thinker by nature and continues to be.
   (B) He used to have positive thinking, but he doesn't have it any longer.
   (C) He was negative, but his personality has changed for the better.
   (D) He was negative, and he has remained unchanged.

5. **What is the main cause of many conflicts?**
   (A) A strong conviction that they themselves are right.
   (B) A strong conviction that there is no absolute truth.
   (C) A frequent change of international laws.
   (D) A frequent change of commercial laws.

II. Sentence Completion

Adjectives（形容詞）

Choose the best answer as a synonym of the word(s) given in the bracket.

1. Japanese people consider an attempt to conquer nature to be _____. (excessively self-important)

   (A) arrogant   (B) assertive

   (C) articulate   (D) artificial

2. People can't take any _____ measures to put out wildfires. (having benefit)

   (A) expert   (B) expected

   (C) excessive   (D) effective

3. The young American was concerned with _____ issues. (relating to land and sea)

   (A) environmental   (B) enormous

   (C) enduring   (D) encouraging

4. He has _____ thinking. (looking at the bright sides)

   (A) plus   (B) positive

   (C) optimal   (D) optional

5. We need to explore a way to make a _____ contribution to the global community. (very important)

   (A) sharp   (B) serious

   (C) significant   (D) similar

「プラス思考」を英語で表現すると？

たとえば、「プラス思考」という和製英語を直訳して、"plus thinking" と表現してしまうかもしれませんが、自然な表現は **"positive thinking"** となります。アメリカなど新しいことに挑戦して失敗から学ぶことを奨励する文化では、失敗の経験を将来どのように活かすかが大切になります。例えば、ベンチャー・ビジネスで失敗しても、「事前に徹底的に市場調査をしておくべきだった」ことを学べば、プラス思考で考えて、

"This is a positive experience for me. I learned that I should do a thorough market research in advance."（これはプラスの経験です。事前に徹底的に市場調査をしておくべきだということを学びました）と表現することができます。

III. Composition

Practice organizing your ideas based on what you have learned through reading. Remember that each person has different opinions and you have to give a detailed explanation.

1. What have you learned through reading about conflict?

ex. I have learned that we are apt to think we're absolutely right.

[Points for improvement]

Apply what you have learned to your past experience.

[The revised answer]

I have learned that we are apt to think we're absolutely right. When a classmate didn't return a CD I had lent him, I had a quarrel with him. At that time, I assumed that it was totally his fault. However, now I'm aware that I should have mentioned the deadline in advance, and told him about that. Starting now, I will let a person in a similar situation know about the deadline beforehand.

[Notes] quarrel: 口喧嘩　deadline: 締切り

2. Give one incident where you had a conflict with someone and think about how you could have reconciled with that person.

IV. Discussion

Practice expressing your opinions clearly. Have your own discussion using the sample below as a reference.

1. **What have you learned through Japanese anime?**

> **Sample discussion**
>
> **A:** What have you learned through Japanese anime?
> **B:** I have learned a lot through the works of Osamu Tezuka who is called a god of comic books.
> **A:** What specifically have you learned?
> **B:** I have learned a lot about philosophy. His works are filled with philosophical elements because he was familiar with diverse fields from medicine to Buddhism.
> **A:** Your statement has made me realize that a lot of input is necessary to increase our creative output.
>
> **[Notes]** philosophical elements: 哲学的な要素　**Buddhism:** 仏教

2. **In one current issue, how can people concerned reconcile with one another?**

> **相手の経験を具体的に尋ねる時の表現**
>
> 相手の経験を具体的に聞きたい場合、別の課で紹介した、**"Can you give me a specific example?"**（具体例をあげてもらえますか）以外に、
> **"What specifically have you learned?"**（具体的に何を学んだのですか）と質問することもできます。いろんな質問の仕方に通じておきましょう。
> 同時に、相手の発言を自分の言葉で言い換えてまとめると、相手の満足度が高まることも覚えておきましょう。

Chapter 13

Applying Cultural Differences to Tasks

異なる価値観を理解することが困難なのは事実ですが、その価値観の差異をお互いの弱点を補う形に活用することもできます。たとえば、企業における製品の共同開発などで優れた成果を上げることが可能です。しかし、価値観が異なるために、事前の取り決めがとりわけ重要になることも覚えておきましょう。

Readings

A Japanese engineer living in the United States stated some merits concerning collaboration on products with Americans. "I have collaborated with American engineers on the development of various products. Americans in general can come up with large-scale projects. However, they aren't good at paying close attention to product quality. When it comes to completing 5 quality products, Japanese and Germans are recognized as superior." Another engineer who did research on dementia shared his experiences. "I belong to an engineering department. While the medical department does research on how to prevent the progression of dementia, our engineering department is developing glasses that can assist people suffering dementia by using AI 10 effectively. We need someone who can invest in our ideas so that we can put them to practical use, but we have difficulty finding that person. We will ask an American to give a presentation at a conference in the United States and find someone to invest in our ideas. The United States has a lot of people called angel investors who are willing to take a chance investing in ideas if they think 15 the ideas are worth the risk."

Also, a Japanese in a managerial position whose work ranges from product development to marketing states, "Even when we develop new products, we have difficulty marketing them in Japan. Take the worldwide hit, Pokemon GO, for instance. It was first marketed in the United States. It made a hit right 20 away. Then, it was introduced in Japan as an American hit item, and it became a smash hit also in Japan. A lot of Americans are fond of novel things. In contrast, many Japanese take a cautious attitude."

As the above statements indicate, the merits of Americans are offering large-scale projects, daring to take risks and conducting effective public 25 relations. On the other hand, the merits of Japanese are paying attention to the details, exercising caution in passing judgment and persevering with product improvement. When collaborating with Americans, it will be more and more important to negotiate with them over what role each participant should play and how the benefits should be distributed. It is a common rule in the global 30 community that we should make arrangements in advance to avoid getting upset when a problem arises.

Notes

l.2 **collaboration:** 共同開発 / l.2 **collaborate with:** ～と共同開発する / l.5 **pay close attention:** 最新の注意を払う / l.6 **superior:** 優れている / l.7 **dementia:** 認知症 / l.9 **progression:** （認知症の）進行 / l.11 **invest in:** ～に投資する / l.15 **angel investors:** エンジェル投資家（創業時あるいは創業間もない企業に出資する投資家） / l.15 **take a chance:** 思い切ってやってみる / l.17 **managerial position:** 管理職 / l.19 **Pokemon GO:** ポケモンゴー（スマートフォン向けのアプリ） / l.22 **smash hit:** 大当たり / l.25 **dare to:** 思い切って～する / l.25 **public relations:** 広報活動 / l.27 **details:** 詳細 / l.27 **persevere with:** ～を忍耐強くする / l.30 **be distributed:** 分配される / l.31 **get upset:** 慌てる

I. Reading Comprehension

Questions are based on the content of the text. Choose the best answer.

1. **What merits did the first engineer find when collaborating with Americans?**
   (A) Americans can draw up detailed projects.
   (B) Americans can pay careful attention to details.
   (C) Americans' ideas are on a grand scale.
   (D) Americans have quality products in mind.

2. **What research did the second engineer do?**
   (A) He researched the development of glasses that can help people's eyesight.
   (B) He researched the development of glasses that can help the brain function.
   (C) He did research on limiting the progression of dementia.
   (D) He carried out research on the cells that cause dementia.

3. **What is easier to do in the United States compared with Japan?**
   (A) It is easier to find someone who has practical ideas.
   (B) It is easier to find someone who can invest in new ideas.
   (C) It is easier to find someone who values research on dementia.
   (D) It is easier to find someone who utilizes artificial intelligence.

4. **What is the point of the Japanese manager's statement?**
   (A) Pokemon GO should have been marketed first in Japan.
   (B) If Pokemon GO had been marked first in Japan, sales would have increased.
   (C) Pokemon GO was first marketed in the United States, and it worked very well.
   (D) It doesn't matter where items are first marketed if the items are novel.

5. **What is not mentioned as items to be considered when collaborating with Americans?**
   (A) To decide how the benefits should be distributed.
   (B) To spend much time talking about each person's role.
   (C) To make arrangements beforehand.
   (D) To spend time discussing religion.

II. Sentence Completion

Adverbs and adverbial phrases（副詞と副詞句）

Choose the best answer as a synonym of the word(s) given in the bracket.

1. Americans _____ can offer large-scale projects. (mostly)

    (A) in general   (B) in particular

    (C) in detail   (D) in common

2. One engineer tried to use artificial intelligence _____ when dealing with dementia. (successfully)

    (A) practically   (B) effectively

    (C) instantly   (D) actually

3. Pokemon GO made a hit in the United States _____. (immediately)

    (A) rightly   (B) right on

    (C) right away   (D) soon

4. A lot of Americans pursue novel items. _____, Japanese people don't. (however)

    (A) In contrast   (B) In comparison

    (C) In detail   (D) In common

5. We have many items to decide on _____. (beforehand)

    (A) in detail   (B) in advance

    (C) in common   (D) in reality

単語は文脈で使い分けを！

たとえば、"soon" を「すぐに」だと思って使う人も多いですが、"soon" は文脈によって「すぐに」や「そのうち」などと意味が変わります。そのため、問題文のように「すぐにご注文をお持ちします」の「すぐに」は **"right away"** や **"at once"** を用いて、**"I'll bring your order right away / at once."** としましょう。なお、この英文では、"take" を使うと別の所に持っていくというような意味合いになるので、"bring" を用いることも覚えておきましょう。

III. Composition

Practice organizing your ideas based on what you have learned through reading. Remember that each person has different opinions and you have to give a detailed explanation.

1. What have you learned through reading about products?

ex. I thought that Pokemon GO was first marketed in Japan, but I have learned that the product was first marked in the United States.

[Points for improvement]

Explain what the fact indicates.

[The revised example]

I thought that Pokemon GO was first marketed in Japan, but I have learned that the product was introduced into Japan after it became a hit in the United States. This indicates that Americans prefer innovative products more than Japanese people.

2. What have you learned through reading about collaboration?

IV. Discussion

Practice expressing your opinions clearly. Have your own discussion using the sample below as a reference.

1. One's merits and demerits are two sides of the same coin. For example, many Japanese are not willing to take risks. Seen from an opposite viewpoint, they are cautious. Give other specific examples.

   [Notes] One's merits and demerits are two sides of the same coin.: 人間の長所と短所は同じ硬貨の裏表、つまり人間の長所と短所は表裏一体であるということ。

> **Sample discussion**
>
> **A:** Do you have experience realizing that one's merits and demerits are two sides of the same coin?
> **B:** Yes, in my workplace some employees consider the store manager as impatient while others regard him highly.
> **A:** They regard him as an efficient worker, right?
> **B:** You have guessed it right.
> **A:** It's always difficult to pass fair judgment on others, isn't it?

2. Share your knowledge of inventions or investments through books or the Internet.

   [Notes] inventions: 発明　investments: 投資

> **発言の推測ができる場合 right を使って確認を！**
>
> 文脈から相手の言いたいことが推測できる場合、Sample discussion のように、**"They regard him as an efficient worker, right?"** と言及し、文末に "right" を使って内容の確認ができます。確認された側は、相手の推測が当たっていた場合、**"You have guessed it right."**（図星ですよ）と相手の洞察力を称えましょう。

<table>
<tr><td>Chapter
14</td><td>*What We can Learn from
Developing Countries*</td><td> </td></tr>
</table>

発展途上国へ、海や陸の自然の豊かさの保護や、貧困層の援助を目的として行ったはずの先進国の人々が、逆に発展途上国から学んだと明言しています。彼らは、発展途上国から何を学んだのでしょうか。

Readings

Many people assume that developed nations are more advanced than developing countries in all aspects. However, some people who have experience living in or visiting developing countries have been positively affected by people in developing countries. Let's listen to what they say.

A French-American expressed his distinctive opinions. "French people in 5 general think only about themselves, so I prefer people in developing countries to French people. I went to Africa several times for technological guidance such as teaching them how to grow vegetables effectively to tackle the food shortage and how to cut trees legally to prevent illegal deforestation. Then, they not only expressed their gratitude but also tried to share their scarce 10 food with me. Their spirit touched me deeply." British people who visited Africa for sightseeing also mentioned the African people's spirit of sharing. "African people have never enjoyed material prosperity, but they lead a happy life by sharing what they have with their neighbors. That attitude was really impressive to us." 15

The above people have different nationalities and purposes when traveling in developing countries, but they have one thing in common: They are impressed with the spirit of sharing. Alfred Adler, a famous psychologist in Austria points out that true happiness has much to do with the conduct of giving something to others. He is said to have given advice to patients 20 suffering depression: "You can be healed of depression if every day you begin the first thing in the morning to consider how you will bring real joy to someone else." Whether or not people have this spirit of sharing seems to be closely related to the fact that while developed nations have many patients suffering depression, developing countries have few cases of patients suffering 25 depression.

Also, an American mentioned. "Americans have pursued material prosperity up to now, but we have to revise this attitude. When I was a child, I used to live in a developing country because of my father's work. I was amazed at the fact that people looked happy with a minimum of comfort. At the same 30 time, I realized that we have wasted resources. After I came back to the United States, I first thought about recycling plastic bottles I had collected on the beach. I now ask companies or NPOs to take cellphones apart I have picked up, and to take out important metals. There are many metal parts that can be recycled."

The present benchmarks of classifying nations into developed and 35 developing nations are employed only in terms of economy and technology. This categorization is questionable if we take into account the degree of happiness and coexistence with nature.

Notes

l.7 **technological guidance:** 技術指導 / **l.9 legally:** 合法的に / **l.9 illegal deforestation:** 違法な森林伐採 / **l.10 scarce:** 乏しい / **l.13 material prosperity:** 物質的な豊かさ / **l.30 minimum of comfort:** 最小限のもので満足すること / **l.31 resource:** 資源 / **l.32 plastic bottles:** ペットボトル / **l.33 NPOs = Non-profit organizations:** 非営利団体 / **l.35 benchmarks:** 基準 / **l.35 classify:** 〜を分類する / **l.37 categorization:** 分類 / **l.37 take into account:** 〜を考慮に入れる

Exercises 14

I. Reading Comprehension

Questions are based on the content of the text. Choose the best answer.

1. **What do many people assume with regard to developed nations and developing countries?**
   (A) Developed nations are advanced no matter what viewpoints people have.
   (B) Developed nations are only more advanced economically and technologically.
   (C) The position of those countries is now being reversed.
   (D) The position of those countries will be reversed in the future.

2. **What cultural difference did the French-American find between French and African people?**
   (A) French people give priority to themselves, but African people don't.
   (B) African people give priority to themselves, but French people don't.
   (C) French people value human relationships while African people don't.
   (D) African people have a strong sense of duty while French people don't.

3. **What did British people discover in Africa?**
   (A) They need material prosperity in order to gain happiness.
   (B) They have to keep pursuing material happiness.
   (C) People can be happy with a minimum of comfort.
   (D) People can be happy if they have a philosophy.

4. **What is the point of Alfred Adler's statement?**
   (A) Find something you can really enjoy.
   (B) Find a calling you can pursue throughout your life.
   (C) Focus on ways to please yourself every day.
   (D) Focus on ways to please someone else every day.

5. **What does the American do now?**
   (A) He encourages people in the developing country to recycle many items.
   (B) He tries to recycle plastic bottles in cooperation with other organizations.
   (C) He tries to recycle important metals in cooperation with other organizations.
   (D) He tries to recycle as many items as possible by himself.

II. Sentence Completion

Nouns（名詞）

Choose the best answer as a synonym of the word(s) given in the bracket.

1. They expressed their _____ to me for my teaching. (thanks)

   (A) gratitude   (B) gravity

   (C) gratuity   (D) grease

2. Their _____ touched me deeply. (action)

   (A) aim   (B) aid

   (C) conduct   (D) habit

3. They brought real _____ to me. (blessing)

   (A) try   (B) trial

   (C) discovery   (D) joy

4. What is your _____ of coming here? (intention)

   (A) goal   (B) purpose

   (C) objective   (D) alternative

5. I came here for _____. (looking around)

   (A) sight   (B) sightseeing

   (C) signal   (D) stay

渡航目的の告げ方と聞き方

外国の空港で出入国管理職員に "What is your purpose of coming here?" と目的を聞かれたら、すぐに **"I came here for sightseeing."**（観光で来ました）、**"I came here on business."**（ビジネスで来ました）と答えられるようになっておきましょう。留学の場合は、**"I came here to study in the university."** や **"I came here to attend a study program."** と答えます。また国内の観光地で、訪日観光客に尋ねる場合 "What is your purpose of coming to Japan?" では硬いので、**"Did you come to Japan for sightseeing?"**（日本に観光でいらしたのですか）や **"Is this a sightseeing trip?"**（観光旅行ですか）が自然な言い回しです。

III. Composition

Practice organizing your ideas based on what you have learned through reading. Remember that each person has different opinions and you have to give a detailed explanation.

1. What have you learned through reading about developing countries?

    ex. I have learned that people in developing countries are happy with a minimum of comfort.

    [Points for improvement]

    Mention how that discovery affects your ways of thinking.

    [The revised example]

    I have learned that people in developing countries are happy with a minimum of comfort. I have begun to doubt that the pursuit of material prosperity will bring happiness to people.

    ....

    ....

    ....

    ....

    ....

    ....

    ....

    ....

2. What have you learned through reading about depression or patients suffering depression?

    ....

    ....

    ....

    ....

    ....

    ....

    ....

    ....

IV. Discussion

Practice expressing your opinions clearly. Have your own discussion using the sample below as a reference.

1. Alfred Adler says: "You can be healed of depression if every day you begin the first thing in the morning to consider how you will bring real joy to someone else." Share your experience bringing real joy to someone else. If you don't have that experience, organize your idea about how you could have brought real joy to someone else in your past experience.

Sample discussion

A: Do you have experience bringing real joy to someone else?

B: Yes, as a birthday present for a friend of mine, I selected a sweater after considering her favorite color and design.

A: That's the spirit.

B: She expressed her happy feelings by saying, "You remembered my favorite color and design. I appreciate your thoughtfulness." I was pleased to hear that.

A: Your experience has made me realize that it is important to come up with ideas that will benefit everyone.

2. Share your opinion about depression. Or you can share your knowledge of depression through books or the Internet.

相槌を打ち、相手の発言をさらに引き出しましょう！

相手の発言を聴いて感心した場合には、Sample discussion のように **"That's the spirit."**（いい心掛けですね）と相槌を打ったり、あるいは似たような経験がある場合は、**"I've got a similar experience."**（私も似たような経験があります）で始めて、あなた自身の経験を語りましょう。そして、最後に相手の経験についての感想や経験の共有を自分の言葉でまとめるのが効果的です。

Chapter 15 | What We Learn from Community Project

スマホを長時間使うとマイナスの影響があるとの研究結果があります。しかし個々人の努力のみでそれを是正するのは容易ではありません。あるコミュニティーでは地域住民が協力して取り組みをしているそうです。どのような取り組みなのか、見てみましょう。

Readings

It has been quite a while since the research was made public that the overuse of smartphones negatively affects the human brain. Nevertheless, addiction to smartphones is a grave issue common in developed countries. In each family even when parents have set a rule with their children to limit the use of their smartphones, the children use them secretly. This has had little 5 effect.

In order to cope with this problem, an American made a viable suggestion. She has told me that she put a large box on a busy street and has encouraged community members to put books families have finished reading into that box. "Even when children shorten the time of using their smartphone, they don't 10 know what to do with that free time. We need to come up with alternative plans. For that purpose, I utilize books presented and persuade the children to find reading enjoyable. I have them return the books and reuse them one after another." At first parents have to choose books which interest their children and get them to read. Once children have discovered the pleasure of reading, they continue reading on their own initiative.

When asked, "What will you do if some children aren't taken care of by their parents?" she replied, "We can expand the concept of family. Community members can treat those children like family members." When asked further, "Most Americans value individualism. Don't they give priority to themselves?" she responded, "That's true. We call it the Me generation. The trend is getting stronger and stronger year by year, so assistance from community is indispensable for those children."

She told me that the above project has brought about synergistic effects. First, children who have acquired patience through reading don't act on impulse. They seldom resort to violence. Community members talk about books they have read and that has promoted more conversations with one another. As a result, community members have begun to pick up trash on streets and plant trees on holidays so that they can improve the environment. Public order in that community is conspicuously favorable unlike other areas where gun shootings are frequently reported.

Notes

l.3 **addiction to smartphones:** スマホ依存症 / **l.7 viable:** 実現可能な / **l.16 on their own initiative:** 自主的に / **l.20 individualism:** 個人主義 / **l.20 give priority to:** 〜を優先する / **l.21 Me generation:** 自分を優先する世代 / **l.24 synergistic effects:** 相乗効果 / **l.25 act on impulse:** きれる / **l.26 violence:** 暴力 / **l.31 gun shootings:** 銃乱射事件

I. Reading Comprehension

Questions are based on the content of the text. Choose the best answer.

1. What do the results of research on smartphones' effect indicate?
   (A) The positive effects are stronger than the adverse effects.
   (B) The adverse effects are stronger than the positive effects.
   (C) The positive and adverse effects are fifty-fifty.
   (D) The effects depend on each child.

2. What suggestion did the American make?
   (A) Parents should set a limit to the children's use of their smartphones.
   (B) Parents and their children should talk about the children's time using a smartphone.
   (C) Parents should ban their children from using their smartphone on weekdays.
   (D) Community members should provide children with used books.

3. What is an accurate description of children's attitude?
   (A) They soon began to read on their own initiative.
   (B) At first parents had to choose books for their children.
   (C) Parents gradually learned to choose books appropriate for each child.
   (D) Children's attitude remained unchanged.

4. How does the American treat children who can't get attention from their parents?
   (A) She urges their parents to pay more attention to their children.
   (B) She introduces an appropriate counselor to each child.
   (C) She encourages community members to treat those children warmly.
   (D) She asks children's teachers to choose books appropriate for each child.

5. What beneficial effect on reading is not mentioned?
   (A) Children have become indifferent to smartphones.
   (B) Children have acquired patience.
   (C)) Children seldom fight with one another.
   (D) Community members interact more with one another.

II. Sentence Completion

Adjectives（形容詞）

Choose the best answer as a synonym of the word(s) given in the bracket.

1. Research on the overuse of smartphones was made _____. (be publicized)

   (A) prompt   (B) progressive

   (C) prospective   (D) public

2. Addiction to smartphones is a _____ issue common in developed countries. (serious)

   (A) global   (B) grave

   (C) gross   (D) groping

3. She made a _____ suggestion. (practical)

   (A) vibrant   (B) viable

   (C) visual   (D) vicious

4. Parents need to come up with _____ plans. (having options)

   (A) alternative   (B) alert

   (C) alike   (D) alive

5. Assistance from the community is _____ for children who can't get much attention from anyone. (essential)

   (A) inspirational   (B) instant

   (C) insistent   (D) indispensable

代替案を提示することの重要性

代替案は英語で **"alternative plans"** と言いますが、英語で意見を交わす時は、相手の意見に対して、常に代替案を考え、提示するようにしましょう。英語圏では学業でも仕事でも議論することが欠かせませんが、批判のための批判（**criticism for the sake of criticizing**）は評価されていません。相手の意見に対する自分の代替案を提示してこそ、人は建設的な批判（**constructive criticism**）とみなします。議論する時には、代替案を常に意識しながら進めましょう。

III. Composition

Practice organizing your ideas based on what you have learned through reading. Remember that each person has different opinions and you have to give a detailed explanation.

1. **What have you learned through reading about smartphones?**

   ex. I have learned that smartphones negatively influence our brains as well as our eyesight.

   [Points for improvement]
   Mention how the fact affects your attitude.

   [The revised answer]
   I have learned that smartphones negatively influence our brains as well as our eyesight, so I have decided to cut down on my emails to friends.

   ....

   ....

   ....

   ....

   ....

   ....

   ....

   ....

2. **What have you learned through reading about the community project?**

   ....

   ....

   ....

   ....

   ....

   ....

   ....

   ....

   ....

IV. Discussion

Practice expressing your opinions clearly. Have your own discussion using the sample below as a reference.

1. Share your opinion about the benefits of reading. If you seldom read, organize what benefits you can expect from reading.

> ### Sample discussion
>
> **A:** Do you often read books?
>
> **B:** Yes, I especially like novels. Through reading novels, I have vicariously experienced the characters' feelings and have become more familiar with human psychology.
>
> **A:** You've got a point there, but I personally prefer non-fiction to fiction because non-fiction deals with what has happened to us and I feel it is closer to reality.
>
> **B:** I understand what you're saying, but when I enter an imaginary world, it relieves my stress more easily.
>
> **A:** After all, there is no accounting for taste, is there?

2. What other community projects can you think of?

> ### 反論の前に、異なる意見を受容する態度を示しましょう！
>
> 相手と異なるものの見方を提示する時には、まず **"You've got a point there, but..."** （あなたの言うことには一理ありますが…）と相手の意見を受け止めてから、自分の意見を言うと、円滑な議論につながります。また、以前取り上げた **"I understand what you're saying, but ..."** （あなたの言わんとしていることは分かりますが…）という形も使えます。**"There is no accounting for taste."** （人の好みはそれぞれです）という諺も押えておきましょう。

読んで発信！ SDGs!

©2024 年 1 月 31 日　第 1 版発行

検印
省略

編著者	小林　純子
英文校閲	Brian Bond
発行者	小川　洋一郎
発売所	株式会社 朝日出版社

101-0065　東京都千代田区西神田 3-3-5
電話（03）3239-0271
FAX（03）3239-0479
e-mail: text-e@asahipress.com
振替口座　00140-2-46008
組版・Office haru ／製版・錦明印刷

乱丁、落丁本はお取り替えいたします
ISBN 978-4-255-15717-7 C1082